HYPNOTISM

by
WALTER B. GIBSON

GROSSET & DUNLAP
A NATIONAL GENERAL COMPANY
Publishers · New York

A Castle Books, Inc. Edition
Distributed To The Trade
By Book Sales, Inc.

CONTENTS

1
MIND OVER MIND

BELIEF in the power of mind over mind dates back to remote antiquity. From then on, it has been demonstrated so convincingly, through century after century, that it has been attributed to some mystic power or supernatural force, an idea which is still widely accepted. For today, this remarkable faculty is known as hypnotism and it is regarded as an approach to the miraculous. How close it comes to attaining that goal depends upon the self-assurance of the hypnotist, the reaction of the individual who serves as his subject, or the gullibility of the witnesses.

Often, all three factors are involved. This was true in ancient Egypt, where the wizards of the pharaoh's court caused lions to follow them about in docile fashion. That depended simply on the wizard's ability to "stare down" a lion, which seemed really superhuman—to anyone who

1

had never tried to stare one down. Other Egyptian sorcerers threw down rods that were transformed into living serpents; this, too, was done hypnotically by applying pressure behind the serpent's head and putting it into a cataleptic state that rendered it rigid and immobile, to all appearances a stick.

Hypnotism played an even stronger part in ancient Greece. There, the oracle at Delphi was presided over by a prophetess known as Pythia, who went into a trance and babbled incoherent messages that were translated as predictions involving the fate of nations. At Dodona, the rustling leaves of a sacred oak, the ringing of a brass tripod struck by metal-tipped whip-lashes that wavered in the wind, and the rippling rhythm of a gushing fountain, were all regarded as divine whispers and were interpreted accordingly. Still more spectacular was the Oracle of Trophonius, where visitors who came for advice were confined in caves from which they emerged in a somnambulistic state and recounted nightmarish visions that they had experienced.

Group hypnotism was predominant in the ancient Roman revels such as the Bacchanalia and the Saturnalia, where the participants gave way to unbridled pleasures and passions, each striving to outdo the other. This phase of hypnotism can be traced progressively through the centuries, because it still continues to exist in varied forms and stages among primitive tribes throughout the world, ranging to higher degrees among more civilized nations.

The war dances of the American Indians, the throbbing tom-toms of the African jungles, the incessant dancing of the Madagascar women while the men of their tribe were away at war, all represent a form of hypnotic persuasion which has found its counterpart in far more civilized lands. European tradition is replete with accounts of dancing manias from the Middle Ages on. One well attested case occurred in Erfurt, Germany, in the year 1237, when a hundred or more children were seized with convulsive spasms and danced their way to Arnstadt, twelve miles to the south, where they collapsed completely, some dying on the spot, while the rest never fully recovered from the effects of the mad epidemic.

Another such case was recorded in Utrecht in the year 1278, when a mad dance spread among two hundred people, who fought off all efforts to break it up. They managed that by confining their convulsive capers to a bridge, which finally gave way under the tramp of their increasing numbers, plunging them into the river, where many of them were drowned. That, perhaps, was fortunate, for there was no telling how far the mania would have expanded if they had spread out through the town and countryside.

That fact was proven nearly a hundred years later in the German city of Aix-la-Chapelle. In July, 1374, people began dancing madly in the street and the frenzy grew to fantastic proportions. The dancers whirled in a wild delirium, screaming and foaming at the mouth. Some collapsed through sheer exhaustion, while others succumbed by beating their heads against walls, until the rumor spread that the dancers were possessed by demons. That, far from curbing the mania, only served to swell it. Troops of dancers, accompanied by equally frenzied musicians, cavorted from town to town, gathering new recruits faster than they could fall by the wayside.

HYPNOTISM

Exorcism was tried to drive away the demons and it succeeded in some cases, which in modern terms would signify that the dancers in question snapped from their hypnotic state. But the majority kept on and the craze became an epidemic, taking over such towns as Cologne, Strassburg and Metz, as well as spreading into the Netherlands. Some people joined the dancers in a spirit of revelry, leaving their homes and shops in order to share the fun, so at times the mania took on the sheer abandon of an ancient Roman festival. But many of the fun seekers were themselves caught in the convulsive swirl and wound up dead or demented before the fantastic craze had run its course.

The dancing mania can be classed as a true hypnotic phenomenon because it had none of the physical or organic factors that characterize a communicable disease. Unlike the black plague and other scourges of that era, it was strictly a mental epidemic. That was emphasized a century or so later, by another dancing mania that broke out near Taranto, Italy, and not only spread widely, but continued to be violently recurrent over a prolonged period of years.

This consisted of a wild, hysterical malady attributed to the bite of a species of tarantula, a large hairy spider found in that locale. Since the tarantula's bite was supposed to be deadly, persons who were bitten were apt to break out in frantic convulsions, thinking that they were doomed. Actually, such bites, though very painful, were not venomous, so the spasms, instead of turning into death throes, eventually subsided and the victim soon recovered. So the convulsive reaction came to be regarded as an antidote for the supposedly poisonous bite.

4

Whether the bite itself triggered the victim's mad behavior, or whether the reaction was instinctive, nobody apparently knew or cared. Either way, it counteracted the imaginary poison and the more a person jumped or danced about, the surer the cure, unless the sufferer collapsed and died through physical exhaustion. Such cases were blamed on the spider bite, increasing the absurd notion that the incessant dancing was a symptom rather than a cure.

Soon, the malady became contagious. Seeing or contacting anyone in that mad dance could start another imaginative person doing the same thing. It might be traced to the superstition that someone shaking off an affliction would cast it, along with the demons that caused it, on to someone else. The origin of Tarantism, as this hysterical outburst is termed, is too obscure to decide the matter exactly. Most important was the fact that the craze spread even more wildly than than the earlier dancing mania.

But in this new wave, group hypnotism figured all the more strongly because it had more to work with. Mere mention of spidery tarantulas touched it off in other parts of Italy. Its recurrence, rather than being merely inter-mittent, was somewhat continuous. Special music was created to excite the victims to even wilder effort, until it became a tonic in its own right. From that developed a wild frenzied dance, accompanied by excited, spirited music, that is still known today as the tarantella.

In contrast to such spontaneous cases, there are those in which group hypnosis is purposely induced, even though the participants may not be fully aware of it. Among Mohammedan nations there are certain mystics

5

known as dervishes; and two of these groups are stand-outs in the field of hypnotic fervor. One group consists of "whirling dervishes," who work themselves up to a su-perhuman pitch by a frenzied, spinning dance; the other is composed of "howling dervishes," who cut themselves with knives, eat live coals and chunks of broken glass and handle red-hot metal with impunity.

Of the howling dervishes, it has been rightfully said that hypnosis and auto-hypnosis, conscious and uncon-scious, have played a part that cannot be over-estimated. At their leader's command, they have been known to lie in the path of his horse and let him ride roughshod over their bodies; yet none showed any sign of pain and all claimed to be unharmed.

Similar marvels were performed by Algerian ascetics known as Marabouts, who concluded their frenzied ritu-als by swallowing thorns, nails and even serpents along with broken glass. They also licked red-hot iron with their tongues, thrust daggers through their cheeks and walked on sword blades, all at the command of their chief, known as the Mokaddem. These feats were wit-nessed and described more than a century ago by a fa-mous French stage magician, Robert-Houdin, who was almost completely baffled by these demonstrations, be-cause he overlooked the hypnotic factor entirely.

That was not surprising, as hypnotism still had not come into its own, hence its full possibilities were not recognized at the time. So Robert-Houdin attributed the feats to crude trickery, even concocting explanations so ridiculously inadequate that anyone reading them would believe that the Marabouts had performed real miracles. But such was not the case. Actually, their demonstrations involved simple scientific principles, a few of which Robert-Houdin recognized, but it was through long schooling in auto-hypnosis that they were able to withstand ordeals or risk frenzied feats from which even hardened warriors would have shrunk.

There was method in all this madness. The Marabouts offered these demonstrations as proof that they were immune to enemy weapons and even gunfire, and that they could confer that same power upon others who believed in them. That enabled the Marabouts to stir Algerian tribes into revolt against French authority, though they never put their immunity to the full test. Rather, they were satisfied to maintain their established prestige through continued control over the mass minds of the tribesmen.

To show how far mass hypnotism can go, we must switch from Algeria to the American West. There, in the year 1870, an Indian named Wodziwob had visions of an impending millenium in which his people would regain their lost lands, yet still continue to enjoy the benefits that had accrued through civilization. To speed the cause, Wodziwob called upon the Indians to invoke the ghosts of their departed ancestors, hoping that they would prevail upon the Great Spirit to come down to earth and preside over the promised happy hunting ground.

The principal ritual was called the Ghost Dance and when it failed to produce results, Wodziwob's sway faded. But nearly twenty years later, the Ghost Dance was revived on a more elaborate scale by a visionary named Wovoka, the son of one of Wodziwob's followers. It was not enough merely to invoke the ancestral ghosts;

by stepping up the tempo of the dance, they could be raised from the dead to share in a land of plenty where the buffalo would roam as of yore and all vestiges of civilization would be banished forever.

Once touched off, the new ritual spread with the speed of a prairie fire, furnishing positive evidence of how auto-hypnosis generates its own self-delusions. While Wovoka, in Nevada, was having new visions promising a peaceful realization of the millenium he had foreseen, members of more remote tribes, notably the Sioux of Dakota, were placing warlike interpretations on his earlier prophecies. They relished the return to earth of their ancestral warriors, for they could picture a horde of such braves driving unscathed through a hail of bullets to annihilate whole troops of United States cavalry, as efficiently as Custer's command had been wiped out by Sitting Bull at the Battle of the Little Big Horn, a dozen or so years before.

So the Ghost Dance took on the character of a War Dance and the participants began having visions of their own. They saw themselves riding along with the ghostly horde, wearing shirts decorated with fanciful designs and symbols that would grant them the same immunity to gunfire. So they painted "ghost shirts" that corresponded to their dreams and the result was a mass uprising. Sitting Bull was killed while being placed under arrest; and many Sioux were massacred by soldiers at the so-called Battle of Wounded Knee, where their painted shirts proved useless, all the result of mass hypnotism on a widespread scale.

In Tibet, it works just the opposite. There, instead of being swayed by the utterances of a lone prophet, the

Buddhist monks, or lamas, choose a human target and concentrate their mass mind upon him. Such a person is called a sungma, and is supposedly possessed by demons, who give him superhuman powers which the lamas can control through a mental force. To demonstrate this group hypnosis, the lamas chant, ring bells and blow horns, while beseeching the demons to take over. Suddenly, the sungma goes into a frenzy and becomes a living oracle, shrieking messages from the spirits, seizing swords and bending them into spirals, along with other superhuman feats which presumably no mortal could ordinarily perform.

Here again, the power of mind over mind is evidenced, this time including a definite physical accomplishment, which is amazing even to those involved, who therefore associate it with the supernatural.

As an example of how rapidly group hypnosis can take over, consider the ritual of walking barefoot over beds of red-hot coals, which for many years was performed semi-annually by the priests of a Shinto temple in the Kanda quarter of Tokyo. How far auto-hypnosis was responsible was something of a question where the priests themselves were concerned. They were trained in the Shinto ritual and the fire-walk also has a physical explanation with which they may have been acquainted; namely, that if the coals are allowed to burn until an ash forms on top, it forms a protection against burns when pressed down by the feet of the fire-walkers.

But mass hypnotism is the logical explanation for the events which frequently followed such fire walks. Onlookers, impressed by the immunity of the Shinto priests and believing that they could share it, would shed their

9

sandals and rush to the bed of coals, following the procession its entire length, without experiencing any harm. Men, women and children all joined these confident throngs, with some of the women carrying infants through the rising smoke from the glowing path. They were told that by joining the ritual, they would be protected from all harm during the coming year; and that was all they needed to take the immediate risk.

Factors other than hypnotism must be recognized where group behavior is concerned. The Bacchanalia was primarily a wine festival, honoring Bacchus, God of the Grape, and many drunken revels have been patterned after it. There is a marked similarity between certain stages of intoxication and hypnotism, such as amenability to suggestion, immunity to pain, lapse of memory, and in the group phase, imitative activity, notably off-key choral singing.

The same applies with narcotics and drugs, for since time immemorial, various herbs and roots have been used to rouse individuals to states of ecstacy or fervor. Evidences of hypnotic similarity is found with drugs that produce hallucinations, perceptual distortions and loss of time sense. Most striking of all are those drugs known as "placebos" which have little or no real physical or pharmacological effect, but which fully satisfy patients who suppose them to be a medicine. Many fake remedies come under this head and once they capture public imagination, it becomes mass hypnotism all over. Indeed, one of the commonest of hypnotic tests is to give a subject a spoonful of water and have him imagine that it is some form of bitter medicine.

So it is not really necessary to travel to distant lands or

revert to ancient times in order to observe the effects of group hypnotism. Sometimes, it has an almost instantaneous effect, a striking example being back in 1938, when Orson Welles put on a radio show based on *The War of the Worlds* by H. G. Wells. To give it dramatic realism, the script was treated as a series of newscasts, with descriptions of men from unknown planets landing all over the eastern United States. So vivid were the reports that thousands of listeners took them literally, never thinking of checking the source of the broadcast. Telephone lines were jammed with calls to police and army posts, while some persons became so frantic that they committed suicide.

That was mass hypnotism on a remarkable scale, with countless individuals tuning themselves to the same false notion and conforming to practically the same reactions, though there were instances where small groups of radio listeners shared one another's apprehensions and built upon their own interactions.

Akin to that, but of much longer duration and far-reaching in scope, was the sighting of "flying saucers" which reached a peak in the 1950s and has been with us ever since. Much has been written and said regarding these Unidentified Flying Objects, or UFOs, as they are commonly termed, but if they actually do exist, the number of times they have been sighted must be few indeed, compared to the thousands of false claims. In the opinion of the noted psychiatrist, Dr. Carl Jung, the vast majority of the reports were results of sheer imagination stimulated by universal fear of nuclear destruction.

That adds up to the equivalent of mass hypnotism, and since Jung's time, the sightings of UFOs have increased

11

and will probably continue indefinitely. But all past crazes were utterly dwarfed by the grooviest expression of the mass mind ever recorded, when nearly half a million rock-and-roll fans converged on a 600-acre alfalfa farm near Bethel, New York, to participate in the Woodstock Music and Art Fair, aptly described as the "ultimate pop experience," which took place over a week-end late in August, 1968.

Thousands of cars were abandoned on traffic-jammed country roads, people died and babies were born in open fields where the flower of American youth wallowed and revelled in the mud more happily than the hogs that had been displaced. When the smoke of the "pot" had cleared sufficiently to find and gather up the remaining debris, it was commonly agreed that there had never been anything like it, before or since.

So the only thing was to outdo it, by staging a later "rockfest" on December 6th, where 300,000 participants strewed themselves and tons of empty wine bottles all over the hills near Tracy, California, in what proved to be the biggest one-day musical "bash" of all time— until then. For the age of mass hypnosis is still with us and in terms of modern tempo, the frenzy of the tarantella would be as staid as a courtly minuet.

2

THROUGH MESMERISM TO HYPNOTISM

THE question "What is Hypnotism?" has produced a great variety of answers, running the gamut from the ancient belief in demoniac possession to the modern claim that the entire subject is an outright fraud. Actually, there are still persons who hold to those respective extremes, though their arguments carry little weight today, but in between there are solid, well-formulated theories, all deserving due consideration, though none affords an absolute explanation.

Perhaps one theory applies to certain cases; another theory to others. Or composite factors may be involved, with one operating almost to the exclusion of the others, under different conditions. The fact remains that hypnotism, in a very definite sense, is quite as nebulous and difficult to isolate as it ever was. So a good starting point toward its analysis is to trace its evolution through the years, showing how different findings have overlapped one another, even to the point where some discredited theories have come back in vogue.

The ancient Greeks invoked sleep by appealing to a god called Hypnos, from whose name the word "hypnotism" was coined many centuries later. The link is quite appropriate, for in ancient Greece, if a person went into a deep sleep or trance condition from which it was difficult to arouse him, it was logically assumed that Hypnos had taken control over that unfortunate individual. So even that far back, there was a discernible difference between natural and hypnotic sleep. The Romans had a similar god named Somnus, who was blamed for inducing odd forms of sleep; hence the modern term "somnambulism" is used to signify sleep-walking and also to denote a hypnotic state that resembles it.

During the centuries that followed, the phenomenon now known as hypnotism was viewed with superstitious awe as a form of witchcraft. It became identified with the "Evil Eye," a baleful, malevolent glare deemed capable of bewitching, injuring or even killing an unfortunate victim by as little as a passing glance. Children and animals were regarded as particularly susceptible to this dreaded power, so charms and amulets were used as protection against it.

In the early 1500s, Henry Cornelius Agrippa, a German physician and scholar, wrote three volumes on *Occult Philosophy*, in which he discussed the art of fascination, as this supposed power by then was known. Agrippa claimed that the instrument of fascination was a subtle vapor generated within the fascinator and projected from his eyes like rays. These were picked up by the eyes of the recipient, who thereby became imbued with whatever mood the fascinator chose to cast.

Contagious diseases, freak accidents, even sudden death could all be attributed to this force, which frequently was blamed, even though the person projecting it was never identified. Love and fear could also be projected by this process, which accordingly had beneficial as well as baleful aspects, according to the mood of the projector. Agrippa regarded fascination as a form of "binding," a power which could halt thieves in their tracks, calm a raging tempest, or render a blazing fire harmless.

Agrippa, far from advocating outworn superstitions, was trying to reconcile them with the scientific thought of his day. He cited the magnet, or lodestone, with its ability to attract iron, as proof of affinities between other objects, great and small. He claimed that gold drew properties from the sun, being of the same color and brilliance, while silver, with its pallid lustre, gained its virtue from the moon; while other metals, as well as gems, were similarly related to various planets.

That set the pace for Paracelsus, an even more famous physician of the same period. He regarded magnetism as an effluence radiating throughout the universe, so that all objects were mutually affected. He assumed that man was infused with an inner spirit, with his physical body representing an outer envelope. This inner man himself had a magnetic power, drawn from the stars and planets, with which he could control other persons and cure their ailments.

In fact, Paracelsus was so successful in his curse, that during the next two centuries, his vague and somewhat visionary doctrines were solidified and extended by later students of the subject. An early Belgian scientist, Johann van Helmont, was perhaps the first to stress the power of will in directing the so-called magnetic fluid, around the year 1600, and his claim to fame as a physicist as well as a physician was proven by his discovery of carbon dioxide.

Another pioneer in this peculiar field was Robert Fludd, a well-traveled Englishman who dabbled in alchemy and other mystical fields. He added a "positive" and "negative" factor to the magnetic theory, claiming that when two persons meet, their reactions will be one or the other, arousing friendliness if positive, antagonism if negative.

How far Fludd was right or wrong is still a question, but there are many people today who think of "personal magnetism" in active or passive terms, and it is a simple fact that personal affinities or antipathies are often established at a first meeting.

A Scottish physician, Robert Maxwell, added still finer points to the magnetic theory around the year 1670. He agreed that the influence of the stars was basic and predominant; but having poured that universal spirit into the individual, it gave him power to project it to persons at a distance, as well as those immediately at hand. Thus, three centuries ago, Maxwell anticipated in a rather primitive way, two very commonplace items of today: ESP (extrasensory perception) and TV (television.)

Meanwhile, magnetic healing was being demonstrated in a very practical way. In both England and France, an ailment known as the "king's evil" was regarded as curable if the sufferer was touched by the monarch's own hand. Hundreds of persons were reputedly healed by that procedure, though statistically they may have been a very small percentage of the many thousands who sought and received the remedy.

One noteworthy feature of this ceremony was the gift of a "touch-piece" in the form of a gold coin or medal stamped with the figure of St. Michael, which the receipient could wear on a ribbon, as token of the cure. This was a direct link to the use of charms and talismans, which not only warded off the evil eye, but in this case helped to dispel the king's evil.

The medals themselves provided a "Heads I win, tails you lose" formula, where the king was personally concerned. If the sufferer's condition improved, the amulet was a constant reminder that the king's touch was responsible; conversely, if the cure failed, the touch-piece could be blamed for not retaining the virtue with which the king had imbued it. Either way, the theory of sympathetic attraction, or lack of it, still followed the precepts set by Paraceleus and his successors.

When Oliver Cromwell became Lord Protector of England, following the execution of King Charles I, he dismissed all efforts to revive the monarchy as "little fiddling things," and would have nothing to do with curing the king's evil. This greatly distressed an Irishman named Valentine Greatrakes, who finally had a vision in which he was told that he had the power to cure many ailments by means of prayer and touch.

Almost overnight, Greatrakes filled the existing void and more. Popularly known as "the stroker," he proved so successful at curing the king's evil that he began stroking away a great variety of other diseases, drawing such crowds of people that he eventually set up shop in London, where his fame became even greater.

His system was to stroke the afflicted area in the direction of the patient's arms or legs, thus working it toward the fingers or toes and carrying the ailment completely from the body. Under such treatment, patients either felt or imagined that that their fingers and toes went completely numb; and as Greatrakes continued his strokes, they frequently became hysterical before returning to normalcy to find the numbness gone and the ailment as well.

After a few years, during which Greatrakes actually cured contagious diseases with his magnetic methods, his power ended as suddenly as it had begun. Though Greatrakes had probably never heard of Paracelsus, or even Fludd, his work furnished what seemed absolute proof of the magnetic doctrines that they had formulated. But the law of sympathetic attraction was even more graphiccally demonstrated by another man in London, at almost the same time; namely, an English adventurer named Sir Kenelm Digby.

Paracelsus had actually applied magnets to the bodies of patients to draw out disease, with occasional success where highly susceptible persons were concerned; hence the stroking process used by Greatrakes was a direct extension of that system. But Paracelsus had used other remedies as well, including salves and ointments, to which he attributed the same magnetic qualities but of a more subtle sort. However, since the attraction could work at any distance—as evidenced by the control of planets over the lives of men—it was necessary to break the influence once for all.

Thus, if the application of an ointment did not heal a wound, there was no need to switch to a different remedy, as we would do today. Rather, the same ointment could be applied to the weapon that had caused the wound, thus blocking off the mutual attraction from the other end. Fantastic though this might seem, all the followers of Paracelsus went along with it; and it remained for Sir Kenelm Digby to establish it as fact.

Sir Kenelm came up with a preparation that became known as "Digby's sympathetic powder" which supposedly contained vitriol and might have caused a burning sensation if applied directly to a wound. Instead, Digby applied the powder to a bandage which had been taken from a wound; never to the wound itself. Actual cures were attributed to Digby's sympathetic powder and though some may have been coincidental it is probable that many were furthered by impressions created on the minds of imaginative persons.

Both Greatrakes and Digby flourished during the early 1660s, and by then the English monarchy had been restored under King Charles II, who promptly renewed the ceremony of curing the king's evil, including the distribution of touch-pieces. It reached a new peak during the reign of his successor, James II, until he was ousted and forced into exile. When William III, a hard-headed Hollander, took over the English throne, he dismissed the power of royal healing as nonsense and actually recommended that people go to France, where James II was living, and ask him to cure them.

Some did and found that though James had lost his throne, he had retained his royal touch, for a whole array of remarkable cures were attributed to the exiled

19

king in his later years. The practice was continued by his son and grandsons as claimants to the British crown and many believers apparently benefitted thereby. But it was never taken up by the Hanoverian kings who succeeded William III, so the custom came to an end in England.

Unquestionably Robert Maxwell knew of the cures effected by Greatrakes and Digby, which could have helped to shape his theory of a universal spirit that could operate at any distance. But Maxwell could hardly have gone along with the claim that Greatrakes drew evil spirits from the persons whom he stroked; nor would he have attributed some special virtue to the sympathetic powder used by Digby. During the next century, both science and medicine made such noteworthy progress that even Maxwell's concepts roused skepticism; so it was not surprising that the next great example of magnetic healing should represent a throwback to the Middle Ages.

About the year 1760, an obscure German priest named Johann Gassner was stricken with severe pains that seemed totally unexplainable until he read a book on exorcism, or the casting out of devils. Suspecting that some demon had taken possession of his body, Father Gassner proceeded to exorcise it and immediately the pains ceased. So he tried it on other people and gained the very same result. From then on, such treatments became his great mission; and though he always spoke to his subjects in Latin, which they did not understand, they usually responded to his commands, raising a hand or an arm, going into a coma or convulsion. He would then order the devils to begone; and frequently, a cure resulted.

Where Greatrakes had gradually expanded the ailments that he treated, Gassner apparently began with the conviction that his exorcisms could cure anything, but soon found that it worked with some diseases but not others. Firm in the conviction that he was invoking divine aid, the good father came to the conclusion that there were two types of illness: Natural ailments, which could be cured by natural means, such as medicines and treatments recommended by physicians of that period; and unnatural ailments, which were obviously due to the presence of evil spirits.

To decide which was which, Gassner applied a sure test. He turned the power on and off. He commanded the evil spirit to depart, return, and depart again. If it responded accordingly—as indicated by the reactions of the patient—he was sure that he was right and that he had banished the demon forever, along with the unnatural disease. If the formula didn't work, the disease was natural, and it was up to the physicians to study the problem and solve it for themselves.

One physician did exactly that.

His name was Franz Anton Mesmer and he had unquestionably delved into the magnetic theories as advocated by Paracelsus onward. But being practical minded, Mesmer was particularly interested in the diseases which Father Gassner had classed as unnatural. Today, they would be regarded as nervous afflictions or chronic disorders of a recurrent type; and Mesmer already had such inklings when he began his medical practice in Vienna in the year 1765. Moreover, he had a distinct advantage over earlier advocates of animal magnetism. Experimenters like Benjamin Franklin had made great strides in the study of electricity, classing it as "positive" and "negative," identifying it with lightning and literally drawing it from the clouds.

After ten years as a magnetic healer, Mesmer met Father Gassner, noted the similarity in results between exorcism and magnetism, and expanded his own theories accordingly. By then, some of his supposed cures had created great controversy among the physicians of Vienna, most of whom opposed his methods and denounced his claims. So he went to Paris and opened a clinic there, summing up his theories in twenty-seven propositions or assertions, which boiled down to the following claims:

A responsive influence exists between the heavenly bodies, the earth and all forms of animate nature, depending on a subtle universal fluid, so widely diffused that it admits no vacuum. Though subject to mechanical laws not yet determined, this action produces alternative effects of flux and reflux, the latter being general, special or compound according to its particular causes.

The properties of matter and organic substances depend upon this universal action and its effects on the animal body result from its insinuation into the substance of the nerves. Thus human bodies display qualities resembling those of the magnet, with its opposite poles, with even the phenomenon of declination being observed, leading to the adoption of the descriptive term of "animal magnetism."

Such action may be communicated to other animate or inanimate bodies, though both classes vary in susceptibility; and the action may be strengthened or diffused by such bodies, as experiments have shown a diffusion of matter, subtle enough to penetrate all bodies with little loss of energy. It also takes place at a remote distance, without the aid of any intermediary substance.

As with light, it is increased and reflected by mirrors; it is communicated, propagated and increased by sound; its magnetic virtue may be accumulated, concentrated and transported. However, some animated bodies have an opposite property that can destroy all the effects of magnetism upon others; and the same rules apply to this positive opposite virtue.

Magnets themselves are susceptible to animal magnetism, so the principle of animal magnetism differs essentially from that of mineral magnetism, showing that the magnet and artificial electricity have properties common to many natural agents where diseases are concerned and any useful results produced by these are due to animal magnetism.

Hence this principle will cure nervous diseases directly and other diseases indirectly. From it, the physician is enlightened regarding the use of medicine and can improve its action, thus provoking, directing and completely controlling any salutary crisis. From this new theory of matter, he may judge with certainty the origin, nature and progress of the most complicated diseases, thus hindering their development and curing them without exposing the patient to dangerous and troublesome consequences. In this way, the art of healing may be brought to absolute perfection.

HYPNOTISM

Though Mesmer's propositions sounded much like double-talk, they had a note of prophecy as well. Such things as x-rays, radio waves or radar were unknown at that time, yet today could be regarded as proofs of Mesmer's fanciful claims. In practice, he put on a show that was spectacular indeed. At his clinic in Paris, Mesmer used a great tub which he called a *baquet*, which was set in the center of a curtained *salon*, with thirty or more persons grouped about it. The tub contained bottles filled with "magnetized" water, stacked in rows and covered with powdered glass and iron filings to make the magnetism still more potent.

Pliable rods ran from the *baquet* to the patients, who were linked with cords passing around their bodies, and they also joined hands, thus enabling the magnetic force, or effluvia, to flow all the more readily throughout the entire group. Soft music played from beyond the surrounding curtains, while Mesmer, attired in a cloak of purple silk, walked about, touching people with a long iron wand, which he occasionally laid aside, while he magnetized patients with his gaze, instead, or made equally effective strokes or passes. At times, he was accompanied by assistants, who also carried iron wands and applied them to the bodies of the patients, particularly those parts which ailed them most.

This claptrap produced a chain reaction that was truly stupendous. Mesmer, as he had artfully mentioned in his propositions, gave definite precedence to patients with nervous afflictions; hence his mere suggestion that a magnetic or electric current was flowing through the group played so strongly on their hair-triggered imaginations that immediately they felt its supposed influence.

They began to gasp and moan; their eyes went shut, their legs gave way, and some seemed to suffocate.

The music, instead of quieting them, only increased their spasms. Hysterical laughter and weeping came from throughout the group and the actors in the mad scene began to view one another as figments of their own fancy. One person might embrace another rapturously, as though recognizing an old friend; others would stare at their neighbors in horror, as though they were fiends incarnate, with horror showing on their own faces as they thrust such persons away.

Although some of Mesmer's subjects remained calm and experienced nothing, observers noted that the great majority were agitated and tormented by convulsions which were remarkable for their number, force and duration, which in some cases continued for more than three hours. Those were featured by involuntary jerking movements of the limbs and the entire body, rolling of the eyes, heaving of the breast and stomach muscles.

Any slight noise caused persons to give a sudden start and any change in the tempo of the music would bring a similar response from many of the subjects, except for those who had fallen into a stupor, as some invariably did. In such cases, Mesmer could instantly arouse the subject by a spoken word, a glance, or even a gesture. From this, even critical observers were inclined to agree that Mesmer, as the magnetizer, possessed some great force that acted upon his patients and gave him mastery over them.

Mesmer termed the convulsive state a "crisis" and when repetition made the patients more violent, they were removed to a special room, where Mesmer gave

25

them more personalized treatment, gazing steadily into their eyes, making magnetic passes with his hands, and sometimes pressing a person's hands between his own, or stroking their heads, shoulders and bodies. All this had a powerful effect upon his patients, who came in such throngs that he had to establish four *baquets*. Finally, to handle the tremendous overflow, Mesmer magnetized a tree in a public square, so that people could attach themselves to it with ropes that served as conductors of the all-healing current.

Whether or not Mesmer fully realized it, he was combining about every method ever used to control the human mind, from fascination to group hypnosis with all stages of hysteria thrown in. His music smacked of jungle tom-toms, the convulsive actions of his patients resembled the dancing manias, his use of the wand excited the awe of Medieval sorcery, while his strokes and passes rivalled the miraculous touch of Greatrakes, Gassner and their royal predecessors. But the effect was so much more spectacular, the results so instantaneous and on so grand a scale, that Mesmer's work was convincing, not only to the general public, but to a small coterie of physicians, among them Charles d'Eslon, whose clientele included members of the French royal family.

D'Eslon studied with Mesmer and not only learned and used his methods successfully, but formulated his own theories on animal magnetism which summarized and clarified some of Mesmer's more obscure precepts. D'Eslon maintained that all ailments were actually one illness, for which there was one treatment and one cure. He claimed that people should be naturally healthy,

hence nature itself endeavored to counteract any func
tional problems. The result was the convulsive crisis that
Mesmer induced.

In D'Eslon's opinion, the medical profession was
wasting its time in giving each type of crisis a particular
name in terms of individual diseases, which thereby became innumerable. Since the cause was always the same,
animal magnetism supplied the answer by rousing a
crisis so potent that the proper cure could be applied
without endangering the patient. But the medical faculty at the university in Paris refused to accept D'Eslon's
ideas and physicians generally were not inclined to give
up their established practices and become magnetizers
like Mesmer.

When D'Eslon was threatened with expulsion from
the medical profession if he persisted in his claims, he
countered by petitioning the king to set up a commission of scientists to investigate animal magnetism and
decide the question pro or con. That was finally done,
and the Royal Commission of 1784 included such no-
tables as Antoine Lavoisier, who had helped discover
oxygen, and Benjamin Franklin, the acknowledged electrical wizard of his time. The commissioners visited a
clinic that D'Eslon conducted, witnessed the effect of the
baquet on his patients, and then requested that he give
them a private demonstration, which he unfortunately
did.

D'Eslon magnetized an apricot tree in Franklin's garden and brought one of his patients, a twelve-year old
boy, into the garden, wearing a blindfold. The boy was
taken from one tree to another, with D'Eslon expecting
him to become convulsive when he reached the right

tree. Instead, the boy went into spasms tree by tree, which gave the royal commissioners the very opportunity they wanted; namely, to reject animal magnetism completely and pronounce it as an outright delusion.

In so doing, most of them were signing their own death warrants. Their failure to recognize how far mass hysteria could go showed that they were totally unfamiliar with the unrest of the times. The frantic urge to flock to Mesmer's *baquets* was actually a preamble to the rising foment that was to culminate in the French Revolution. By the time that broke, Franklin was safely back home in the U.S.A., but practically all his fellow-members of the Royal Commission were rounded up and executed as reactionaries. About the only commissioner who survived was a doctor named Guillotine, who later devised a sharp-edged instrument for beheading royalists that still bears his name; and in its own grim way, the *guillotine* proved to be a surer, swifter cure-all for human ailments than the *baquet*.

By using primitive electrometers and other instruments available at that time, the commissioners came up with the unanimous conclusion that "There is nothing to prove the existence of a magnetic fluid; the violent effects observed in patients under public treatment are due to contact, to the excitement of the imagination and to the mechanical imitation which involuntarily impels us to repeat that which strikes our senses."

So far, fair enough, but having thus discredited animal magnetism, the commissioners stepped out of bounds by trying to reject all its phases, as witness their next statement:

"The contact and repeated excitement of the imagination which produce the crises may become hurtful; the spectacle of these crises is likewise dangerous on account of the imitative faculty which is a law of nature. Consequently, all threatment in public in which magnetism is employed must in the end be productive of ill results."

Here, they were going into conjecture of their own, offering arguments as invalid as those of Mesmer and D'Eslon. At one point, they ridiculed the testimony of patients who claimed that they had felt the magnetic emanations. The commissioners laid that to Mesmer's passes, saying that the motion of his hands could have caused a cold breeze, or that the approach of his hands could give off bodily warmth. Here, they were playing safe by ascribing to a physical cause the very results that they had earlier attributed to imagination alone.

The remainder of their findings, including a "secret report," was literally honeycombed with other contradictions, making it obvious that they were really out to get Mesmer; and did. Mesmer left Paris, discouraged and discredited, while French physicians, from D'Eslon down, were threatened with expulsion from the medical profession if they continued to support his theories or practice his methods. That apparently marked the end of animal magnetism, or mesmerism, as it was also styled, in honor—or perhaps more frequently in dishonor—of its originator.

But the lingering twilight of mesmerism was not to fade entirely. It was to dawn anew and gain scientific acceptance under a somewhat different guise and another name: Hypnotism.

3

THE DEVELOPMENT
OF HYPNOTISM

DURING Mesmer's sudden surge to fame, he had asked the French government to finance his remarkable cures and he had been offered a subsidy of 30,000 livres a year, the equivalent of $6,000, a large amount in those days. But Mesmer had demanded a guarantee of 500,000 livres, and when that was not forthcoming, he turned to wealthy patrons instead, forming an organization called the Society of Harmony to establish magnetic centers throughout France, with trained practitioners paying him a share of their fees.

Among the subscribers was the Marquis de Lafayette, whose name alone brought in other liberal members of the French nobility. So when Mesmer's fad died out in Paris, the movement did not have to go underground, as it might today. It simply moved from Paris to the provinces, and among those who carried it there was another nobleman, the Marquis de Puységur. He had paid his fee to learn Mesmer's system and wanted to find out if he had received his money's worth, which he really doubted. So he tried it out in the sticks.

It worked far beyond his expectations. When De Puységur gave a magnetic treatment to a woman to cure her toothache, she sat quietly while it went away. He tried it again, with another woman, and the same thing happened. There was nothing resembling the convulsive crisis that featured all of Mesmer's sensational cures. Instead of driving the patients hysterical, the treatment acted like an anesthetic, rendering them insensible to pain.

Working with a young peasant named Victor Race, the marquis magnetized him into a quiet sleep which was followed by a delirium in which Victor fancied himself at a dance, a shooting match and various other places. The marquis repeated this regularly with the youth and found that the magnetic treatment invariably produced a complete change of personality. From a humble, slow-spoken peasant, Victor became a loquacious youth who chatted with the marquis as a friend and confidant. On one occasion, Victor entrusted the marquis with a valuable paper, asking him to keep it safely for him; then, after being roused from his magnetic trance, the youth spent all the next day looking for the document and wondering what he could have done with it.

The Marquis de Puységur and his brother concentrated on this phase of magnetism not only with Victor but with other subjects and found that such amnesia, or loss of memory, was easily induced with susceptible patients. As the marquis himself described it: "The line of demarcation is so complete that these two states may almost be described as two different existences. I have noted that in the magnetic state the patients have a clear recollection of all their doings in the normal state; but in the normal state they can recall nothing whatever of what has taken place in the magnetic condition."

De Puységur, like Mesmer, magnetized a tree to serve as a *baquet*, and, again, the results were diametrically opposite. Where excitable Parisians had gone berserk in keeping with Mesmer's fad, the stolid French peasants who gathered around a stately old elm on the village green were lulled into calm oblivion, at the beck or touch of the marquis and his brother. Some 130 local patients were treated simultaneously on one occasion, all with quieting effects.

Helping to lull them was a bubbling spring at the foot of the tree, which most of them had known since childhood; as young folk, they had danced around that tree on summer evenings; when older, they had gathered beneath its shade to discuss crops and other local matters. By joining them in their familar gathering place, the De Puységurs gained their absolute confidence and thus induced the results they sought. When the marquis proudly stated, "The tree is the best *baquet* possible; every leaf radiates health and all who come experience its salutary influence," he was speaking for himself and his brother as well as the assembled peasantry.

The whole secret of magnetism, according to De Puységur, depended upon the simple formula, "Believe and Will." When his trusting subjects believed that they could will themselves into the happy state that the marquis promised, they did exactly that; while the marquis, believing that he could so control them, brought his own will into play, with mutually remarkable results.

De Puységur's chance discovery of the trance condition, with its resultant amnesia, not only opened up new vistas for magnetic experimenters, but brought Mesmer's earlier and more limited work back into respectability. Unfortunately, the expansion of the field also gave credit to Mesmer's theory of an electrical effluvia, something which few physicians or scientists were inclined to recognize. But the trance condition was rated as genuine, even though the operators who induced it had mistaken notions regarding it. From the De Puységurs on, they termed it "somnambulism" because of its close resemblance to sleepwalking, which was already a known phenomenon.

When a French physician, Desire Petetin, magnetized certain subjects into a state of catalepsy, wherein their muscles remained rigid or immobile, it strengthened the interest in somnambulism. The induction of hallucinations, both positive and negative, and the carry-over of suggestions from the somnambulistic state into the waking stage, along with various lesser phenomena, all supported this more advanced concept of animal magnetism. The varied factors included a built-in time sense, the apparent ability to describe distant scenes or future events, and to diagnose ailments in the subject's own body or someone else's.

How much of this was simply due to heightened imagination on the part of a subject or exaggerated claims made by the operators, as well as observers, was as debatable a question as the source of the so-called magnetism itself. Many magnetizers preferred to experiment with highly susceptible patients or subjects, as De Puy-ségur had with Victor. Once conditioned to such tests, a subject not only went into the somnambulistic state with astonishing rapidity, but developed a heightened sug-gestibility that enabled him to anticipate the magne-tizer's wishes and thus apparently respond to unspoken commands.

All this vested somnambulism with a mystique that became increasingly impressive, while other magnetizers so broadened the field that the magnetic influence really seemed to be universal. One notable example was a Por-tugese abbot named Jose Custodio de Faria, who came to Paris from India, shortly after the Napoleonic era, and put on regular demonstrations of somnambulism by selecting a dozen subjects from a larger group and put-ting them into an instantaneous sleep by pronouncing the word *"Dormez!"*—the French for "Sleep!"—in a forceful, imperious tone.

In all, the Abbe Faria put more than 5,000 persons in-to the somnambulistic state by that system, which was far more than enough to dismiss any charges of decep-tion or confederacy, which skeptics of the period contin-ually threw at magnetizers. But to top it, the Abbe Faria disclaimed animal magnetism as the cause, claiming that the results depended upon the reaction of the subject, rather than the power of the operator. This idea was furthered by a French physician, Alexandre Bertrand, but the magnetic theory still held sway.

A Swiss magnetizer named Lafontaine later reduced animal magnetism to basic terms when he eliminated the human element by fixing his gaze upon a caged lion at a zoo in Tours, France, and causing it to fall into a profound sleep. Not only did Lafontaine handle the lion's paw with impunity; he thrust his hand between its jaws and even pricked its nose with a pin. Lafontaine repeated this experiment in Tours, Nantes, and elsewhere, and though he still attributed it to some magnetic influence, he proved that no confederacy or chicanery could be involved, as it would have been difficult indeed to talk a lion into playing the part of a stooge.

Perhaps that stood in Lafontaine's favor when he put on an exhibition of animal magnetism in Manchester, England, in November, 1841. Several local physicians were present, hoping to brand the demonstration as a fake, but one of them, Dr. James Braid, was so impressed by the way the magnetized subjects were unable to open their eyes, and could remain insensible to pain, that he was convinced that Lafontaine had something, even though it might have no relation whatever to magnetism.

So Braid began a series of experiments of his own. He had people gaze steadily at a fixed object and found that it put such subjects into a state of sleep or trance, for which he coined the new term, "hypnotism." Later, Braid modified his technique, because he found that the fixed gaze, when prolonged, could be tiring on a person's eyes; but from the very start, he had proven something to his great satisfaction and that of future experimenters; namely, that no animal magnetism or other projected force was involved.

As the operator, Braid simply instructed his subject on what to do and played no further part. Indeed, there was nothing to prevent a subject from putting himself into a hypnotic state. This marked hypnosis as a purely subjective state, but with different degrees dependent on suggestions given by the operator. These he classed as Slight Hypnosis, in which the subjects became lethargic, but were conscious of what went on about them and could remember it after awakening; Deep Hypnosis, from which awakening subjects remembered nothing of what transpired, unless they were re-hypnotized; and Hypnotic Coma, in which loss of memory of occurences while in the trance condition proved complete and could not be revived.

But at the same time, Braid noted such variations in the suggestibility of his patients, that he decided that the different degrees had intermediate stages that were difficult to define. Hence, in 1860, when Ambrose Liebeault, a French country doctor, began working from Braid's findings, he formed six classifications, ranging from mere drowsiness to deep somnambulism. Liebeault's remarkable cures among the French peasantry won him the support of Hippolyte Bernheim, a medical professor in Nancy, who increased the count to nine degrees, yet at the same time recognizing that each hypnotized subject exhibited his own individuality or special personality. Later, these degrees were again reduced to three by Auguste Forel, a Swiss physician who furthered the findings of the "Nancy School" as represented by Liebeault and Bernheim.

Meanwhile, a rivalry had sprung up between the Nancy School and the Salpetriere School in Paris, which was headed by Jean Martin Charcot, an eminent neurologist, who concentrated entirely upon hysterical patients, on the theory that they alone were truly hypnotizable. Disregarding Liebeault's cases, which outnumbered his own by 1000 to 1, Charcot obtained such fantastic results with his specially selected and utterly responsive subjects that his tests became a veritable throwback to the early days of animal magnetism. At one point, Charcot used actual magnets, something which even Mesmer had rejected; and since hysterical persons were easily thrown into a cataleptic state, Charcot classed it as a common degree of hypnosis, rather than the rarity it was.

The Nancy School eventually won an almost total triumph, which did much to further hypnotism as it is known today; but at the time, established facts were still countered by unreliable conjecture. As an example, Liebeault, Bernheim and Forel all concurred in the opinion that the hypnotic trance and ordinary sleep were basically the same. This claim had double support because suggestions given to persons in ordinary sleep often produced a definite response; and when hypnotized subjects were left alone, they usually awakened as they would from natural sleep.

However, detailed studies conducted from independent and advanced viewpoints over many years, have not only offered conclusive proof that the hypnotic trance differs from natural sleep, but have enabled observers to check the transition from one state to the other. Similarly, other theories that were seemingly well established in regard to various phases of hypnotism have either been amended or disproven, with the way still open for more changes.

As a case in point, Braid, the pioneer in the field, claimed that he had noted a distinct difference between the trance state and ordinary sleep, only to have the authorities of the Nancy School reject his finding as superficial, in the light of their more extensive experiments. Furthermore, Braid had come to odd conclusions later, talking in such terms as "phrenomagnetism," which indicated that he could have been mistaken in some of his earlier observations as well.

Although hypnotism had gained acceptance in medical and scientific circles, its progress still was slow. The few physicians who practiced it confined their work chiefly to patients, rather than the general public; and their methods were mild compared to the old-time mesmerists and magnetizers, who made out best of all. They abandoned their old titles and advertised themselves as hypnotists, which to an extent they were, with the exception of those who were outright fakers. Soon they were riding the crest of a tidal wave, with "hyp acts" appearing at town halls, dime museums, sideshows and over vaudeville circuits.

Some of their work was genuine and most of it was impressive, because to punch up their performances they planted confederates in the audience; and these stooges, known as "horses" in the trade, would come up on the stage when the hypnotist called for volunteers. Some were actually good hypnotic subjects, conditioned to undergo various ordeals. Traveling hypnotists took their "horses" along and supplemented them with accomplices who were hired locally and rehearsed in the parts they were to play. But like the old magnetizers, a good professional hypnotist could always get real results with suitable subjects who came up on the stage. So professional hypnotists continued to impress scientific observers, just as Lafontaine had impressed Braid.

38

4

AUTO - SUGGESTION: A MODERN KEY TO HYPNOTISM

WHEN the French commission dismissed Mesmerism as a conglomeration of suggestibility and imagination, they were acting far less scientifically than they supposed. From their limited viewpoint, it seemed ridiculous even to think that two such nebulous factors could combine to form what Mesmer classed as a magnetic fluid. Yet earlier in that very year of 1784, when the commission was filing its report, an English scientist named Henry Cavendish was proving that he could accomplish in a physical way the very sort of result that Mesmer claimed was possible in a mental or metaphysical state.

At a meeting of the Royal Society of London, Cavendish described how he had pumped the air from a huge glass cylinder and replaced it with quantities of hydrogen and oxygen, which he had touched off with an electric spark. The astonishing result was that the two gases united to form water, always in the ratio of two to one, thus furnishing the famous formula of H_2O, which is one of the first things taught in chemistry today.

Turning two gases into liquid was even more preposterous than turning two states of mind into a fluid, but the French scientists accepted Cavendish's findings because his experiments had been conducted according to their rules, just as they had rejected Mesmer's claims because he had gone by his rules, not theirs. It didn't occur to the commissioners that there might have been a parallel between the two experiments; those dealing with physical elements—as hydrogen and oxygen—and those that involved metaphysical factors in terms of suggestion and imagination. But the emphasis, in the case of hypnotism, still remained upon the physical as much as the purely mental aspects until the year 1910. Then, a French druggist named Emil Coue, who had studied hypnotism under Liebeault, some twenty-five years before, decided to abandon the trance condition and concentrate entirely upon suggestion applied in the waking state.

During his career as a druggist, Coue had come to the conclusion that a patient's mental attitude was often a better cure than medicine. He argued that many doctors employed medicines as a mere remnant of age-old superstition, whimsically backing his claim with the statement that the Rx at the head of every prescription was a form of invocation to the ancient god Jupiter. But Coue did not stop there; he carried his theme still further.

By Coue's logic, the power of suggestion lay in the

mind of the patient, or the subject; and when properly intensified, could stimulate that person's imagination to a degree that would effect a cure, or whatever else might be desired. Hence, in a broad sense, just as Cavendish found that the formula H_2O turned two gases—hydrogen and oxygen—into a liquid commonly termed water; so did Coue supply the formula of S_2I to prove that the proportionate admixtures of two mental states—suggestion and imagination—could produce what then was known as hypnotism, but which today would be properly termed a hypnoidal condition.

Though Coue did not reduce it to such terms, he implied as much, so the analogy between the chemical formula of H_2O and the figurative expression S_2I is both graphic and allowable, though there is no way of determining the exact amounts of suggestion and imagination required with any individual person. But it is proven fact that if those two mental elements are touched off, so to speak, by a spark in the retort of the human mind, a definite metaphysical result will follow.

Addressing himself to the average person, Coue described what he termed a "crucial test," which has since become a classic in its own right, namely:

If a plank thirty feet long and one foot wide should be placed flat on the ground, could you walk along it? Most certainly, you could. But suspend that same plank between the summits of twin towers, two hundred feet above the ground, could you walk along it then? Most probably you would become dizzy before you took two steps and you might even lose your balance and fall to the ground.

From that beginning, Coue developed a whole series of cases, covering human experience and reactions from babyhood up, showing how suggestion was needed to stimulate the equally necessary factor of imagination. A baby, seeing people walk and talk, would imagine that it could do the same, thus gaining those abilities. Later, riding a bicycle, learning to swim, and still more complicated actions, came under the same general head and were cited by Coue as proofs of his case for auto-suggestion.

There is no need to go into the many cases that could be cited. They will suggest themselves and it is easy to imagine the results, exactly as Coue claimed. It should be noted, however, that both positive and negative reactions are evidenced in Coue's system of auto-suggestion. For example:

A person who has learned to dive from a height of five feet might try it from levels of fifteen, thirty and finally fifty feet, thus gradually conditioning himself to higher dives. But if he recognizes his own ability at the start and sees another diver of his caliber diving from the fifty-foot level, he could readily skip the intervening stages and make the high dive with impunity.

Coue stressed such points by frequently reverting to the classic example of the suspended plank, stating that a steeplejack could walk along one because he believed he could, whereas the average person believed he could not. Reducing this to still simpler terms, Coue pointed out that going to sleep at night was actually a matter of auto-suggestion, with a person keeping the thought of sleep in mind; while in contrast, anyone who constantly pictured himself as awake, would be troubled with insomnia.

Referring back to his experience as a druggist, Coue remarked that even the simple act of swallowing a pill could prove impossible for anyone who worried over it; yet that same person, finishing a hurried meal, might inadvertently swallow a plumstone. Through such homely examples, Coue propounded the dictum: "Our actions spring, not from our will, but from our imagination," and set out to demonstrate its truth. He recommended relaxation exercises and simple tests of a self-hypnotic type that until then had been regarded as trivial, but proved convincing to people who first conditioned themselves by accepting Coue's theories.

As a result, a Coue cult sprang up so rapidly that in the early 1920s, Coue left his home town of Nancy, France, and toured England and America, lecturing on his theme of "Self-mastery Through Autosuggestion." A puckish, bearded man in his mid-sixties, he not only found that people liked him, he found them attentive to his doctrine, but he simplified it to the point where it oversold itself.

As a pharmacist, Coue emphasized the curative qualities of auto-suggestion. In turn, that attracted listeners who were suffering from real or imaginary ailments. For them, Coue already had a set formula, which ran, in twelve little words:

Day by day, in every way, I am getting better and better.

That was to be constantly repeated; and if you don't think it will work, try it; but first put yourself in a receptive mood. Coue thereby was supplying auto-suggestion in capsule form, giving people a taste of what was later to become known as the power of positive thinking, as well as by many other names.

Unfortunately, although Coue did not stop with that initial statement, the vast majority of people did. Overnight, it became a catch-phrase that took on the proportions of a cure-all. That, in turn, proved how far auto-suggestion itself can go, for Coue and all he stood for soon became known by that one slogan, which millions of people soon were reciting in parrotlike fashion, regarding it favorable, antagonistically or indifferently, according to individual preference; and thereby missing out on the vital message.

Thousands of believers in Coueism immediately testified to its worth because for the first time in their lives they woke up ready to meet the day's problems and enjoy the day itself, instead of grumbling or moaning themselves into the usual tired feeling that bordered on collapse. Critics, on the other hand, ridiculed it as something that would spring a dislocated joint back in place or grow hair on a bald pate by merely reciting a meaningless jargon. A host of in-betweeners took up Coueism as a form of wishful thinking, only to abandon it as soon as the fad died out, which it did, quite rapidly.

So Coue went back to France, neither sadder nor wiser, but certainly richer and confident that he had accomplished his mission. Among the follow-up methods of his system was this: If a pain persisted after the twelve-word formula was repeated, Coue recommended the old system dating back before the days of Mesmer, that of ordering the pain away with the repeated statement,

"It is going—it is going—it is going—" as long as need be, which he claimed should average a mere twenty to twenty-five seconds, once a person acquired the right tempo.

To give people the needed knack, Coue established institutes in which classes were conducted by his more ardent followers, who not only demonstrated their self-mastery through auto-suggestion, but passed the gift along to others. From these have come many of the hypnoidal experiments described in other chapters, so that hypnotism, as it is commonly practiced and popularly accepted today, owes much of its success to Coue. Though all of Coue's clinics have long since faded from the scene, they have left their mark in many other forms as well. Classes and courses on Perfect Living, Cosmic Power, Psycho-dyanmics, Personal Magnetism, Ways to Influence People, and many other current themes are all based on Coue's fundamentals of auto-suggestion and therefore represent varying degrees of self-hypnosis.

During the semi-retirement that preceded his death in 1926, Coue summarized his theories in the forthright statement, "I am not a miracle man. I do not heal people. I teach them to cure themselves." Among the illustrative experiments which Coue recommended to show how the conscious mind could control the unconscious, was the "pulse test" in which a person endeavored to quicken his pulse beats, slacken them or cause them to become intermittent.

Though hardly a convincing demonstration when attempted by the average person, the pulse test became the stock-in-trade of an Egyptian mystic named Tahra Bey, who did pose as a miracle man, or something close to it.

HYPNOTISM

Tahra Bey, who sprang to fame in Europe at about the time when Coueism was fading out, was able to stop his pulse entirely and perform a variety of other remarkable tests that many scientific observers attributed to self-hypnosis.

One of Tahra Bey's specialties was pushing long, thick steel needles completely through his cheeks and jaws, then withdrawing them and causing blood to flow or stop, according to request. He also laid upon a bed of spikes, so sharp-pointed that touching one with a finger would prove painful, and rested calmly while a 100 pound stone was placed upon his abdomen. Next, the stone was cracked apart with blows from a sledge-hammer, yet Tahra Bey arose unperturbed and showed that his bare neck was not even dented by the formidable spikes.

To top it all, Tahra Bey performed a living burial, in which he was placed in a coffin that was sealed and covered with sand, on the center of a lighted stage. After twenty minutes, the sand was removed and the coffin opened, whereupon Tahra Bey emerged as calmly alive as when he had been sealed in the casket. Tahra Bey advertised this as a feat of suspended animation, similar to an intense trance condition which the yogis of India term *samadhi*, and to prove his claim, he allowed his mouth and nostrils to be stuffed with cotton, apparently making it impossible for him to obtain air during his twenty-minute ordeal.

So powerfully did Tahra Bey impress his audiences, that plans were made to bring him to America, practically to pick up where Coue had left off. But there was a marked difference between the approache of the benign

French druggist who optimistically talked ailing people into making themselves well and that of the poker-faced Egyptian fakir who openly claimed occult powers. Suspecting that the fakir might be a faker as well, newsmen interviewed Howard Thurston, then recognized as America's leading stage magician, on the matter of Tahra Bey. One by one, Thurston explained away Tahra Bey's miracles, as follows:

Stopping the pulse completely could be accomplished by having a small rubber ball concealed in the folds of the fakir's sleeve, just under the armpit. Pressing the arm against the body would cause the ball to cut off the flow of blood, thus reducing the pulse beat practically to zero.

Pushing thin knives and long needles into various parts of the body was simply an old sideshow trick, according to Thurston. Originally, it had been done with fake knives which had blades sliding up into the handles, but in later years, the "human pincushions" as such performers styled themselves, found that various parts of the body were only slightly vulnerable to sharp-pointed implements.

This applied particularly to the cheeks, which had comparatively few blood vessels and therefore could be punctured completely. To cause blood to flow, the fakir had only to pull out the needle rapidly; to prevent the flow, he drew it out slowly, giving the wound time to close itself. Thus, a phenomenon that was attributed to power of the mind was nothing more than a natural physical reaction.

Lying on a bed of spikes was an old yogi feat that Thurston had witnessed often, when he had toured India many years before. The greater the number of spikes, the harder it looked, but the easier it really was, because it meant less weight for each spike. With dozens of such spikes, none received pressure of more than a few pounds, even when a 50-pound stone was planted on the recumbent fakir's chest. Breaking the stone with a sledge-hammer was another sideshow stunt often performed by "strong men." By using a hammer with a comparatively small head, the mass of the stone absorbed the force of the strokes, which were scarcely felt.

As for the living burial, Thurston dismissed that as anything miraculous on the ground that there certainly was enough air in the coffin to last for twenty minutes and that Tahra Bey, being alone and unobserved, could have worked the cotton from his mouth and nostrils, replacing it just before the coffin was opened. Even if his mouth and nose were sealed, he still might have some trick of loosening the bandage sufficiently to gain a steady trickle of air, which was all he would need to breathe slowly and steadily.

All that pointed toward the skeptical reception for Tahra Bey, once he came to America, but as it turned out, he never came. Not that he was worried over the possible outcome; he just happened to be so busy filling European engagements that he couldn't spare the time to tour America. In his stead, another fakir named Rahman Bey came to the United States and began a sensational vaudeville tour, presenting an exact replica of Tahra Bey's act. American audiences ate it up, and Rahman Bey gained added publicity by putting on special demonstrations for physicians and college professors, many of whom were impressed by his work.

One professor of psychology, speaking to his class

after they had witnessed Rahman Bey's tests, summed it up thus: "You have just seen a demonstration of auto-hypnosis, with one person acting both as operator and subject, something so rare that it seems incredible."

Auto-hypnosis was indeed a factor, though it was not so rare as the professor supposed. The lesser tests were the sort that old-time hypnotists had performed with regular stooges or "horses," who were so conditioned to the set routine that they became indifferent to pain. But with the living burial, where he placed himself beyond call or contact, even if only for twenty minutes, Rahman Bey needed a mental formula such as Coue had prescribed and more. That meant auto-suggestion, plus.

To attempt the living burial, Rahman Bey had to *believe* that he could go through with it, and during his interment, *imagine* that he was close to its completion, thus reducing minutes into moments. To let his imagination run riot and stretch minutes into hours, could have caused panic, where the buried fakir was concerned; but instead, he took it calmly, show after show, proving conclusively that auto-hypnosis was involved.

Oddly, it was a contest between auto-hypnosis and mass hypnosis, for as the minutes ticked by, most of the spectators pictured themselves "in there" with Rahman Bey. It was they, not he, who underwent the real ordeal. Always, sentiment favors the underdog, and if he happens to be in a sealed coffin down under a few pounds of sand, more power to him; he needs it. So Rahman Bey won over the entire American public, with the exception of one man: Harry Houdini.

For a quarter of a century, the name Houdini had been a synonym for the miraculous. Known as the

Escape King, he had extricated himself from every form of restraint, such as handcuffs, straitjackets, jail cells, safes, vaults, and even devices of his own invention, which included an oversized milk can and an elaborate contrivance known as the Water Torture Cell, in which he was immersed upside down before the curtains were lowered to give him a matter of mere minutes to free himself or undergo death by drowning.

Nearly all of Houdini's stage escapes were effected within the walls of a curtained cabinet, where he frequently lingered long after he had freed himself, to rouse the audience's excitement to a fever pitch, by making his escape seem more formidable than it was. At one theater, after a rapid routine escape from a packing box in which he had been handcuffed and nailed, Houdini found a trap door which had been used by an act some weeks before. So he went down through the stage and up to the manager's office, where they sent out for sandwiches and coffee. After the snack, Houdini returned below stage, and up through the trap into his cabinet. There, he ripped open his collar, mussed his shocky hair, and reeled out through the curtains, flinging the handcuffs ahead of him, to receive a standing ovation from a wildly appreciative audience that thought he had been fighting to pry his way out of the packing case and shake off those handcuffs all during the past half hour.

In short, Houdini, like the famous P.T. Barnum, was not only a master showman, but a master of humbug as well. Many of his escapes did demand strenuous physical exertion, but in later years, he had eliminated all that were really dangerous in order to take out a sizable life insurance policy. But Houdini's act stemmed from the

50

1890s, when people had been gay but gullible. With the advent of automobiles, motion pictures, airplanes, and all the turmoil and excitement of World War I, people had smartened enough to think in terms of fake handcuffs, special keys or picks, and boxes or trunks with trick panels where escapes were concerned; while every traveling carnival had its "handcuff king" who posed as another Houdini.

So Houdini himself had turned to lecturing on the methods of fraudulent spirit mediums, while planning a big magic show to go on the road in competition with Thurston's. It was at that juncture that Rahman Bey suddenly shot to fame with what was practically a "nothing" act, compared to Houdini's bygone escapes. More than once, Houdini had been forced to fight against time, when air was running short in a vault, or in a packing box submerged in a river. To think of Rahman Bey lying complacently in his coffin, simply waiting to take a bow after they dug him up, would have been rankling indeed to anyone but Houdini, who simply turned it to his own advantage.

Publicly, Houdini denounced Rahman Bey as a fake, declaring that the air supply in the sealed coffin was more than sufficient to last anyone even longer than twenty minutes, provided the entombed person breathed easily and calmly. In response, Rahman Bey not only increased the length of his test, he allowed himself to be submerged in an airtight coffin at the bottom of a Manhattan swimming pool for more than a full hour, emerging as complacently as ever.

That suited Houdini perfectly. He had been practicing in a coffin of his own and felt he could do better than

HYPNOTISM

Rahman Bey. So he put on a public demonstration in a hotel swimming pool and stayed under for an hour and a half. Later, he stated: "There is nothing supernatural in what I have done. I am an ordinary man. You don't have to go into a trance to do this test. The trick is to inhale a considerable amount of oxygen beforehand and store a reserve in the body; then, in the coffin, take short, even breaths. In that way, you conserve the air supply."

Actually, no ordinary man would have gone into that coffin to begin with, let alone be sealed inside it and sunk to the bottom of the pool. But Houdini was an extraordinary man, whose own power of concentration was so intense that it became a form of auto-hypnosis in its own right, though he refused to recognize it as such. Having seen so many fake hypnotic acts in his dime museum days, Houdini wouldn't believe that the genuine article existed. Yet all the while, he was demonstrating it, and the way his name has lived is conclusive proof of the hypnotic power that he exerted over the public mind.

Hereward Carrington, a leading authority on psychic subjects at that time, noted a marked difference between the living burials of Rahman Bey and Houdini. According to Carrington, Rahman Bey pressed firmly upon his forehead with his fingers; then upon his throat with his thumbs. He then threw himself backwards, taking in his breath with a sharp gasp, and dropped into the arms of waiting assistants, who lowered him into his coffin. At the finish, he came out in the same condition; his hands were pulled away from his neck and forehead, and he collapsed into the arms of his assistants. A few moments later, he again became his normal self. In contrast, Carrington claimed that Houdini, when he came from the coffin, was deathly pale, running with perspiration, and with a pulse of 142.

To Carrington, that was proof that Rahman Bey had been in a genuine cataleptic state and that Houdini had put on a spurious exhibition, treating the whole thing as a mere endurance contest. Houdini took the attitude that Rahman Bey had done no more than go through a well-rehearsed act and that if he'd tried to stay submerged as long as Houdini had, he probably wouldn't have come out alive.

Actually, the controversy was never fully settled for shortly afterward Houdini went on tour with his big show, and though he took along a special casket and had lithographs printed to advertise the "Living Burial," he did not add it to the show. Possibly he was waiting for Rahman Bey to try for a new record, so that he could again outdo the fakir. Nobody ever knew, because several weeks later, Houdini succumbed to an attack of acute appendicitis and died in a Detroit hospital, on October 31, 1926.

Early the next year, on January 28, 1927, another self-styled fakir, Hamid Bey, underwent a living burial under strict test conditions in Englewood, New Jersey, and stayed below ground for more than three hours, adding further credence to Carrington's claims that true catalepsy was involved, but causing skeptics to regret that Houdini was no longer available to dispute this new challenger's record.

The person who profited most from all this was Howard Thurston, who promptly added a most spectacular version of the Living Burial to his own big magic show.

HYPNOTISM

Thurston utilized a steel-framed coffin with all its sides made of glass. He gave the throat and pressure treatment to a Hindu assistant and placed him in the glass coffin which was then sealed and immersed in a large tank of water, which also had glass sides.

All during the rest of that act, through an intermission and during most of the next act, the entombed Hindu was thus in full view of the entire audience, eliminating any chance of trickery, such as a secret air tube, as had been suspected in the case of Rahman Bey, or a hidden oxygen tank, which other skeptics hinted that Houdini might have used. The coffin was then raised, the Hindu was removed and revived, quite ready to repeat the test—which ran nearly an hour—in Thurston's next show.

Thurston presented the burial as a cross between an Oriental mystery and a scientific demonstration. He stated that three factors were involved: Trance, Hypnotism and Air Conservation. In signed articles, as well as in his speech from the stage, he stated that there were many cases in which Hindu yogis had lived apparently without breathing for hours, days, and even weeks. He added that there were other cases where people who had been pronounced dead, revived later; and that hypnotism could produce a state that resembled such a trance.

Thurston claimed that if the average man should be confined within the glass-walled coffin, he would consume all the available oxygen within ten minutes, even becoming so worried or restless that he would have to be removed in even less time. The secret, therefore, was to relax, breathe lightly and make no unnecessary movements which, like heavy breathing, would consume vital oxygen. By using someone susceptible to hypnotism, particularly a Hindu, Thurston found that he could induce his subject to assume and maintain a lifeless position, with his breathing so imperceptible that the test might be prolonged indefinitely.

Stressing auto-suggestion as the predominant factor, Thurston recommended such measures for persons trapped in submarines, mines, or other cramped spaces, pointing out that the best way out of a desperate situation could be through passivity rather than activity, where air conservation was most essential. He predicted that this principle would some day save human lives; and with all the complexeties that have developed during the atomic age, he was right indeed. Hypnotists have actually been assigned to submarines, to be ready to calm crew members in emergency; and people who are skittish about taking airplane trips have been induced to fly through hypnotic treatment.

Still more attention was focussed on the hypnotic phase of living burials when a noted writer on occult subjects, Paul Brunton, visited Tahra Bey, the first and foremost of the modern Egyptian mystics, in Cairo, Egypt, and watched him demonstrate suspended animation under the most exacting conditions. According to Brunton, Tahra Bey cut the blood flow by the usual pressure and curled his tongue inward, as though to swallow it, cutting off his air supply as well. His mouth, nose and ears were stuffed with cotton and he was buried in a coffin set in a trough and covered with sand. After the time specified, an hour and a half, he was brought out and restored to life.

Describing his experience, Tahra Bey insisted that

his sleep was so profound that he knew nothing of what had been done to him. He could only recall that he had closed his eyes in the room where he now was, and that by a mysterious process of post-suggestion, he had re-awakened in the same place at the very moment that he had set. Checking back to his European tour of years before, Tahra Bey declared that he had undergone still longer burials while in a cataleptic trance and he produced data to substantiate the statement.

That also spoke well for the claims of Rahman Bey, as opposed to those of Houdini; but it so happened that Houdini's cause was still to have support. Some twenty or more years later—to be exact, on February 7, 1956—a modern escape king known as James "The Amazing" Randi undertook the submerged coffin test in the very hotel pool where Houdini had undergone it nearly thirty years before. Houdini's exact time had been clocked at one hour and 31 minutes, whereas Randi stayed under one hour, 44 minutes and 30 seconds, although a physician in attendance doubted that there was enough air in the coffin to last more than twenty minutes.

Two years later, Randi repeated the test in a swimming pool in London, this time staying under for two hours and three minutes. His coffin was the same size and capacity as Houdini's, but one meticulous critic pointed out that Randi was younger and weighed much less than Houdini had. Since Randi occupied less space in the coffin, it naturally contained correspondingly more air, but certainly nowhere near enough to better Houdini's score by more than a half hour.

The real reason could very well be that Randi, along with being a skilled escape artist and a competent magician like Houdini, was versed in hypnotism as well. Perhaps that gave him just enough extra "something" to prove that all sides of the story had their merit, and that the real key lay in the one vital word: Auto-suggestion.

5

HYPNOIDAL TESTS

PERHAPS the easiest way to recognize the effects of auto-suggestion and observe how it merges into the hypnoidal or light hypnotic state is to make a few standard tests on your own and check the results. You won't have to walk a plank five hundred feet in the air or dive from a sixty-foot tower, spectacular though such feats may be. Instead, you can convince yourself right now, wherever you are, by reading the following instructions one by one and trying each in turn.

The Glued Eyelids: Place the tip of your right forefinger high on your forehead and press straight downward. Raise your eyes and look intently upward as though trying to see your forefinger. Since it is beyond your range of vision, close your eyelids, but still keep looking upward, visualizing the pressing finger by mentally bridging the gap.

As you intensify that process, try to open your eyelids. You will find that you can't; not only do they seem to be glued together, they may become closed even tighter. By removing your finger from your forehead and letting your eyes look downward, the spell will be broken and you can open your eyes with ease.

Here is the reason: The muscular action of looking upward counteracts that of opening the eyelids. Only when you relax that upward strain will your eyelids open. But the strain itself seems to be upon the eyelids. That is a most intriguing feature of auto-suggestion; the result not only draws attention from the real cause, but may be attributed to a totally different source. With experiments that can be further intensified, auto-hypnosis often follows.

In itself, the "Glued Eyelids" may be regarded strictly as a test for suggestibility. Thus it can first be given a quick trial, avoiding any overstrain. Press forehead—look up—close eyes—*try to open lids*—remove pressure—look down—open lids. Do this in a slow, rhythmic count, pausing for a few extra beats on "try to open lids" as that is the real crux of the test. It can be further simplified thus:

Instead of using finger pressure, pick an object well above normal eye level, such as the top of a picture on the wall, a high book shelf, or the edge of the ceiling. If outdoors, use the top of a hill or building. Stare straight ahead, then without lifting your head, raise your eyes toward the chosen target. Whether or not you can quite see it does not matter. Either way, you close your eyes and keep visualizing it while continuing your upward gaze. Try to open your lids; after you fail, look down-

HYPNOTISM

ward and open them as described.

The Clamped Hands: Fold your hands by interlacing your fingers and pressing their tips between the knuckles of the other hand. The thumbs should add a similar pressure, one against the knuckle of the opposite forefinger; the other against the knuckle of the opposite thumb, all as far down as possible. Lower your clasped hands below chin level and keep pressing firmly, bringing the heels of the hands together.

While concentrating on such pressure, try to open your hands. You will find that you can't, and the more you try, the more helpless they will seem. You can watch until your knuckles lose their color under your forceful fingers, yet all strength is gone from your hands themselves. Only when you raise your clamped hands prayerfully and relax completely will they literally slide apart.

The same principle is at work as in the eyelid test. One force is applied against another. What seems to be a mere pressure of the fingers actually keeps the hands from opening in normal fashion, since you are pressing inward against the backs of the hands themselves. Again, relaxation relieves the pressure, and in this case it can be gained automatically as the hands are raised, as any change from a set position brings other muscles into play.

For a really tight hand clamp, lower your hands to waist level and push your forearms straight inward from your elbows. This literally jams the heels of the hands together so hard that even if you lessen finger pressure, you still can't pull your hands apart. In fact, they may seem more helpless than ever.

The Rigid Arm: A third test of your own suggestibility is to raise one arm on a level with your shoulder and make it as rigid as possible. To do this, you take up slack by stretching your arm clear to your finger tips, stiffening them as well and constantly reaching farther outward, until the added distance is imperceptible except in your own mind. You must think of your arm as a steel rod, which doesn't demand much stretch of your imagination, because by now it should feel like one.

Your fingers, like your arm, should be kept straight out, still reaching to an imaginary limit; at the same time, try to lower your arm. The chances are that you can't, for again, you will be retarding one muscular action with another. The more you stretch, the stiffer your arm becomes, because you are concentrating on that one factor; but the moment you relax, it should drop automatically. If it falls too readily, raise your arm and add another stretch, with fingers stiffened as before. If your arm becomes numb, it is all the more likely to stay rigid until you relax.

The Heavy Foot: Stand erect with your feet a few inches apart and lift your left foot straight upward, flexing the left knee a trifle, if necessary. Don't try to lift your foot high; in fact, the less the better, as you are simply trying to prove to yourself how easy it is to raise your foot from the floor or the ground. Keep your body erect as you do this.

Now spread your feet farther apart, say twelve inches or so. Keep your body erect, with shoulders well-squared, eyes straight ahead, much like standing at attention, but without the heels together. Now, maintaining that exact position, try to lift your left foot as you did before. If you proceed as described, it won't come up. Your foot either seems heavy or acts as though it were magnetized to the floor. If you continue the futile struggle, the sensation may shift from your left foot to your left knee, which can still flex, but is unable to raise itself.

Yet once you relax, letting your shoulders droop a bit, while your body sways slightly in relief, your foot is freed from its fixed position and your knee functions as it should. Why? For a very simple reason that you can learn through a further test.

When you stand with your feet close together, you must shift your weight to your right foot in order to raise your left. This, in turn, causes your right shoulder to move to the right, serving as a counterbalance when the left foot is lifted. This is almost imperceptible, until you spread your feet farther apart, as described. Then the shift to the right will force that shoulder to make a distinct dip, unless you keep both shoulders squared, with body erect and hands at sides. By assuming that posture and concentrating upon it, the shift is impossible, and since your weight remains distributed on both feet, you will be unable to lift the left one.

When you relax and forget about your shoulders, the power will come back to your left knee, because as you try to raise your left foot, you will unconsciously shift your weight to the right. To appreciate this subtle principle, you can give it an added test, as follows:

Set the side of your right foot against the base of a wall, with your left foot up to a dozen inches to the left, resting your weight equally on both feet, as already described. Your right arm should be at your side, but you do not have to stand stiffly erect or square your shoulders. Any effort to lift the left foot will fail, because the wall blocks you from leaning far enough to the right.

In this form, the test is somewhat obvious, as you have to step completely away from the wall in order to overcome it.

Summarizing the tests just described, you will recognize that they are quite baffling until you know the secret. Hence if you tell someone to try them, without revealing the principles involved, a susceptible person is apt to believe that some peculiar power, such as hypnotism, is involved. In this, they resemble valid tests for suggestibility, which will be described in due course. The difference is that in the valid tests, a person must be placed in a fully receptive mood, which in many cases amounts to a mild hypnosis. The tests just given do not have to meet that requirement.

Still, the fact that they are actually tricky is somewhat advantageous. They can be used to win over a skeptic to the idea that he can be hypnotized, which is often a very necessary step toward inducing actual hypnosis.

There are various other devices which appear to be hypnotic, yet which actually depend on unsuspected muscular reactions. But most of these definitely involve two persons, one acting as the hypnotist and the other as his subject. Hence they will be described and detailed later, in connection with further hypnoidal or hypnotic tests, which they closely resemble. As with those just described, they can be introduced as "convincers" when stubborn subjects are encountered.

6

HOW TO
INDUCE HYPNOSIS

MODERN methods of hypnotism are many and varied, but they all have one definite purpose; namely, to put the subject, or person being hypnotized, into a responsive mood toward any suggestions made by the operator, or hypnotist. Generally speaking, these methods run to two extremes, dependent on the manner and the mood of both the operator and the subject, as well as the time and place.

If the operator is a domineering, quick-spoken individual, he can easily sway a shy, retiring subject, who is impressed by such tactics; but he will naturally have to lessen his dramatic tone with a subject who refuses to be browbeaten. Conversely, a quiet, persuasive operator can often win a skeptical subject to his way of thinking, but will have to adopt a more forceful manner toward a person who expects something of a dynamic nature.

A stage hypnotist prefers the bombastic style for three good reasons: First, his act must impress an entire audience; second, the volunteers who come up on the stage at his request will often try to show off unless he moves fast to balk them; and finally, once he does gain the upper hand, the glare of the footlights and the presence of an audience helps to subdue them into a responsive mood. That's when a real "pro" with long experience can take over in a convincing way.

Psychologists have the advantage of laboratory conditions or an attentive class of students, with all the time they need and little to lose if a subject proves to be unresponsive. So they find the persuasive approach best suited to their needs. But whenever a stage hypnotist is weeding out the volunteers and finds a highly susceptible person among them, he is apt to switch from his regular routine and put the chance subject into a deep, convincing sleep. Always, he is on the lookout for good subjects for his best tests. By the same token, a psychologist demonstrating hypnosis under laboratory conditions should speed up the action and step up his tone in anticipation of a subject's natural response to his suggestions.

Hence the "varied methods" already mentioned represent "in-between" techniques, which can be combined as needed. These follow well-proven patterns, which will be covered in detail, so that anyone who wants to try them can do so. But it must be emphasized that to become a hypnotist, more than mere method is required. The operator must have confidence in himself and understanding of the subject as well. This personalized relationship was fully observed and detailed by Dr. Au-

HYPNOTISM

guste Forel, as follows:

> A hypnotized subject is not a perfect automaton under the complete dependence of the hypnotist. The dependence is a very relative one, encumbered by all sorts of conditions. Suggestion means a sort of tournament between the dynamisms of two brains: One gains mastery over the other up to a certain point, but only under the condition that it deals skillfully and delicately with the other and does not go against the grain.

That covered the situation perfectly, but Dr. Forel had more to say, concerning the hypnotist's own ability and his choice of methods; namely:

> The best hypnotist is the one who can best convince his intended subjects of his capability of carrying out the hypnotic process, thus inducing a proportionate enthusiasm. Such enthusiasm is important both for the hypnotist and his subject. The hypnotist must be convinced of his own ability, or else possess dramatic talent, to convince others satisfactorily.
>
> But it is the achieved result which induces the greatest enthusiasm both in the passive and the active party to the contract. Everything which fills us with enthusiasm gains power over our brain activities, conquers contrary impressions and suggests to us by means of the stimulation of corresponding plastic pictures of the imagination.
>
> Thus the hypnotizability or suggestibility of a

subject increases with his enthusiasm and his confidence, as well as with the enthusiasm and successes of the hypnotist. Correspondingly, it sinks with mistrust and failures. Other factors also assist, especially individual plasticity and intensity of the impressionability, exhaustion, sleep capability, etc.

Keep those factors in mind when you study the methods that follow. All are based on procedures set and attested by authorities in the field of hypnotism, and while each may be regarded as a technique in its own right, it will be seen that many of their phases are interchangeable. Where one leaves off, another may take over; and most important, whenever a capable operator sees fit, he can inject an individual touch of his own. Such points are noted among the following descriptions.

THE FIXATION METHOD

Fixation was originally regarded as the one sure method of inducing a true hypnotic trance. The procedure was to hold a bright object, such as a key or a button, above the level of the subject's eyes and have him stare upward at it in such steady fashion that his eyes became tired and closed almost of their own accord. This resulted in a drowsiness during which the subject became responsive to suggestions put by the operator, finally awakening at the latter's command.

The fault of this process was its attempt to balance two conflicting elements: concentration and relaxation. If the subject drifted easily from one state to the other, well and good; but often the eyes became overstrained and the experiment had to be abandoned. Either that, or the strain resulted in unpleasant sensations after the subject was awakened.

However, further experiments with highly responsive subjects proved that suggestions could be introduced earlier in the process, thus reducing the fixation period. That led to the use of preliminary suggestions, such as telling the prospective subject what to expect and how he should react; or even letting him witness the effect upon other subjects before his turn was due. These measures were so successful that they proved conclusively that suggestion was the primary cause of hypnosis, with fixation simply an adjunct, yet still essential in cases where the power of suggestion could not be stepped up sufficiently to command a subject's full attention.

One of the strongest advocates of the power of suggestion was Dr. Hippolyte Bernheim, who retained fixation as an adjunct, but utilized the first two fingers of his right hand as the object of attention, instead of a key or a button. Bernheim's procedure, which has been used by many capable hypnotists, runs as follows:

The operator tells the subject that there is nothing strange about hypnotism; that it is like an ordinary sleep which can be induced in everyone. He then says, "Look at me and think of sleep; nothing but sleep . . . . Your eyelids are feeling heavy . . . . Your eyes are tired . . . . Very tired . . . . They are beginning to blink . . . . Your eyes are closing . . . . "

By this time, a highly suggestible person may be closing his eyes. If so, the operator continues, "Closing . . . . They are closed . . . . Tightly closed . . . . " timing his statements to his observations. But if the subject fails to respond with more than a mere flutter of his eyelids, the operator gestures with his right hand, moving his fingers toward the subject's eyes and above their level as he adds:

"Your eyelids are closing .... They are closed .... Tightly closed .... You can not open them .... So tightly closed you can not open them .... Your arms feel heavy .... So do your legs .... Your hands can not move .... You can not feel anything .... You see nothing .... You feel nothing .... You are going to sleep .... To sleep .... SLEEP!"

The final word, timed to the right moment and given in commanding tone, is apt to sway the balance, bringing about sleep or a state closely resembling it. But even if such inclination is lacking, and the subject's eyes remain open, the operator still has an alternative. That is to spread the fingers close to the subject's eyes and gently draw the lids downward in imitation of natural sleep. This is very effective in cases where the subject's eyes have become rigidly fixed, without the lids closing of their own accord.

Keeping the subject's eyelids closed, the operator repeats his verbal suggestion, "Your eyelids are stuck together .... So tightly that you can not open them .... You need sleep more and more .... You can not resist it .... Sleep!" The intonation here is gradually lowered until the final command; and repetition of this formula usually produces sleep or some degree of hypnotic influence. Then, of course, the fingers are drawn away and the eyes remain closed.

It should be noted that with the subject seated comfortably, his—or her—eyes are looking upward at the outset, which in itself is a fixation. This makes it difficult for the eyelids to open, once they have been closed, a fact that was practically unknown in Bernheim's time. This accounts for many successes in the early stages, where the subject, struggling unsuccessfully to open his eyelids, succumbs to the operator's persuasive talk. When the operator later closes the subject's eyelids with his own fingers, he is simply implementing what he should have already accomplished.

This is proven by the next stage.

The operator raises the subject's arm. It remains up-lifted. When extended straight out, it tends to remain rigid. Here, again, muscular strain may play a helpful part, but at this stage the hypnotic influence usually has reached a degree where the subject will automatically follow the operator's commands. Dividing the hynotic state into exact degrees is purely arbitrary, as it varies with different persons. In the early stage, the operator can follow up the eye closure test by announcing: "Your eyelids are no longer heavy . . . . You can open them now . . . . Open them!"—and the subject will respond accordingly.

The same applies with the raised arm test. Once the operator tells the subject that he can lower his arm and even dares him to do so, the subject will have no trouble doing so. These are not necessarily "spell-breakers"; at times, a subject may accept them as further commands while he is progressing into a deeper stage of hypnosis.

The operator watches for such symptoms and takes due advantage of them. Having shown that he can control and release the subject's eyelids, and cause his arms to remain rigid or relaxed, the operator can further stress his earlier suggestion that the subject is powerless to move at all. He can even challenge him on that score, telling him that he is frozen in his chair and can not possibly get up from it. Even if a subject struggles successfully against such a suggestion and finally comes to his feet, the test is quite impressive, because of the real effort involved.

But often such effort fails completely, or the operator is able to interrupt it soon enough to convince the subject that he is really helpless. The operator is then able to move into tests of a more advanced type. Having proven that he can prevent the subject from performing voluntary muscular actions, he now demonstrates that he can make the subject do such actions automatically, under the power of suggestion alone. As an example:

The operator takes the subject's hands and begins moving one about the other. When the operator releases them, he tells the subject: "Go on . . . . Go on . . . . Keep moving your hands . . . . You can not stop . . . . You can not stop . . . . No matter how hard you try!" If the subject keeps on, it shows that he will be amenable to other automatic actions, so the operator continues with other tests suited to this intensified degree. Even if the subject manages to slacken the rotary movement through spasmodic effort, it indicates the deeper stage.

Since we are now dealing with basic methods of inducing hypnosis, deeper stages will be covered later. All preliminary processes lead to those advanced phases, so to encourage them, the operator may press the subject's eyelids from time to time or keep repeating the command "Sleep!" whenever the subject shows signs of awakening

71

too soon. To awaken the subject, the operator commands, "Wake up . . . . It is over . . . . Wake up!" This is usually accepted as a new suggestion and the subject promptly awakens. If his eyes remain closed, the operator can add, "Your eyes are opening . . . . You are awake." Blowing on the closed eyelids also helps if the subject's response is slow.

Just as the sleep suggestions are progressive, so can the awakening be anticipated. This is particularly important when the subject is approaching a deeper stage of hypnosis, as an ordinary awakening may then be too sudden. Anticipation is built in various ways: When repeating the early command to "Sleep," the operator may add, "You are still in a deep sleep . . . . You will not wake up until I tell you to do so . . . . You will only awaken when I tell you." This is very effective when moving from one test to another, as it keeps the subject in a hypnotic state during the transition.

It also gives the subject the progressive suggestion that he is due to awaken later; and the operator can add further anticipation by pinpointing it almost to the moment, saying, "You will wake up in exactly five minutes," or some other specified period. This may lead to an automatic awakening at the end of that interval, as a hypnotized subject's time sense is generally very acute. The operator can also ease the subject into a wakening process by telling him, "I am going to wake you up . . . . I want you to count slowly up to ten . . . . Slowly up to ten . . . When you say 'Ten,' you will be awake. Count up to ten and wake up!"

When the subject responds to such a command, he virtually wakes himself up and usually does not remember having counted at all. Thus a typical "sleep command" has been turned into a "waking command." By way of further anticipation, the operator should occasionally insert the statement, "You are going to wake up very comfortably . . . . Your head will be clear and you will feel perfectly rested." This will relieve any strain that the subject has undergone.

The mere fact that the command to "Sleep!" must be repeated with other reminders shows that there is a constant trend on the part of the subject to awaken of his own accord. Sometimes, this may happen abruptly in the midst of a test or during a transition. Similarly a test itself may fade: A stiffened arm may sag or rotating hands may lag, unless the operator continues to "talk it up." Hence if a subject should refuse to waken promptly from a deep sleep, there is no cause for worry. His trance will lapse into normal slumber and he will awaken naturally in due course.

THE FINGER PRESSURE METHOD

As a modern development of Bernheim's Fixation Method, the following procedure is not only swift and sure, it is specially suited to the dynamic type of operator who represents today's trend. That may be defined as a cross between the professional and the professorial. More important, it is the form of approach that most impresses the intelligent hypnotic subject, the only kind that you really find today.

The operator seats the subject in a chair and tells the subject to look upward. This can be "toward me" or "toward my eyes" or "toward my fingers," meaning

73

those of the right hand, which are directly toward the subject's gaze. But all this is a mere device to draw attention from the more important action of the left hand, which is the vital factor. We may say, quite honestly, that deception helps in this method, which is all the more in its favor, as hypnotism itself is deceptive from start to finish.

In this momentary period of the subject's concentration, the operator says, "Now close your eyes—keep them closed—easily—calmly—still looking toward me." This can be modified by "toward my eyes" or "toward my right hand," either of which keeps the subject in a relaxed condition. This is quite the opposite of the standard procedure which requires an intensive gaze. But that is to come, though indirectly, which is its great beauty. Once the subject's eyes are closed, the operator shifts from a frontal position to the right side of the subject.

During this simple maneuver, the operator keeps his right hand raised in front of the subject's closed eyes, so that if they should open, the subject would be staring directly at the operator's fingerstips, those of the right hand, thus maintaining the fixation already established. Meanwhile, from his new position at the right side of the seated subject, the operator presses the first two fingers of his left hand high up on the subject's forehead and states:

"You can feel my fingers pressing down upon your forehead . . . . Keep your eyes closed and raise your eyes upward . . . . Still higher upward, as if you can see my fingers pressing your forehead . . . . Visualize them, as if you really saw them . . . . "

Already, the operator is cashing in on the first test of suggestibility, the "Glued Eyelids." While this is used as a preliminary in other methods, it carries a special impact in the present case. Just as you can try this simple test for yourself, in this instance the operator can produce the same effect upon the subject. Instead of recognizing the importance of the upward gaze, the subject is completely lulled into an unsuspected situation. The operator follows through with the statement:

"Keep visualizing my fingers.... Now try to open your eyes. You can't.... Your eyelids are glued shut .... Tightly shut.... You are powerless to open them until I give the word.... No matter how hard you try, it will be impossible.... Your eyes are glued shut.... Tightly shut...."

By watching closely, the operator can view the subject's efforts to raise his eyes beneath their closed lids. He stops the flutter of the eyelids by placing his right thumb and fingers gently against them and drawing them downard, while telling the subject:

"Relax.... Don't try to open your eyes.... Just go to sleep.... Go to sleep quietly.... Sleep.... Sleep .... Sleep.... You will stay asleep until I tell you to wake up.... Until then, sleep...."

However the operator may vary these words, he should deliver them in a lulling tone, even thinking sleep as he continues. Thus, without effort, often in a matter of moments, the operator has accomplished a result that usually takes considerable time and strain, both for the operator and his subject. He keeps telling the subject to breathe slowly, quietly, easily and to await his next command. Meanwhile, he draws away his right hand, gradually relaxing the forehead pressure of his left fingers until that hand, too, can be drawn away. He then proceeds with the "Arm Rigidity" test.

In this instance, he not only raises the subject's arm to shoulder level, but draws it toward himself, since he is now at the subject's right. He carries his right hand clear to the subject's fingers, straightening them as he arrives there. While his right hand draws the fingers outward and the arm with them, he brings his left hand to the spectator's right shoulder and draws that hand along the extended arm, encouraging the spectator to stretch it farther. At the same time, the operator intones the suggestion:

"Your arm is stretching farther . . . . Stretching farther . . . . Keep reaching farther . . . . Reach farther with your fingers." Here, as the operator's left hand nears the subject's wrist, the right hand takes over, while the left returns to the subject's shoulder and repeats the drawing motion, as the operator continues: "Your arm is stiffening . . . . Stiffening as you stretch it . . . . Your wrist has stiffened, so has your hand . . . . your fingers . . . . Your whole arm is firm . . . . Firm and rigid . . . . Like a bar of iron . . . . You can not move your arm . . . . You can not drop it . . . . Not until I command it."

This has created the very tension needed for the "Rigid Arm" as described under "Auto-suggestion." Again, the operator has produced a hypnotic effect through his knowledge of muscular reactions. Here, he may add: "While I press your forehead, your arm will stay up . . . . Stay up . . . . Like a bar of iron . . . . " But this is optional, as the operator's actions already suggest it.

To conclude the test, the operator continues: "Now, relax .... Relax your arm at my command .... I command it to move downward .... It is dropping downward." Fitting action to his words, the operator relaxes pressure of his left fingers on the subject's forehead and at the same time rests his right hand lightly on the subject's extended arm, so as to press it downward if response is slow. He times the phrase "Dropping downward" to the actual fall of the spectator's arm.

Since the subject is now relaxed, the operator—if he wishes—may lift the subject's hands and bring them in front of the body, telling the subject to clasp them tightly together. He then introduces the "Clamped Hands" test, which also depends upon muscular reactions combined with suggestibility, as described under "Auto-suggestion." In this case, however, the operator adds some special features which make the test all the more effective.

The operator helps clamp the subject's hands by pressing them between his own hands, telling him, "Your hands are clasped .... You can not open them .... Press tightly .... Tightly .... Hold them .... Hold them .... " Again, the operator is taking advantage of a muscular law, and since the subject is clamping hard of his own accord, the operator carries the suggestion further by bringing his left hand to the subject's forehead and pressing it as he did before, saying, "You can not open your hands until I relax pressure and command you to do the same .... Keep pressing until you hear the command .... Now, I command you: Relax! .... Your hands are coming apart .... Now!"

By relaxing finger pressure on the subject's forehead,

the operator increases the power of the verbal suggestion and the subject, after struggling to separate his hands, finds to his sudden astonishment that he has succeeded.

All this is building to a grand climax, a test in which the subject is rendered completely powerless. Though that can often be accomplished through suggestion alone—as described with other methods—here the operator again has a secret weapon in the form of muscular reaction, though it will remain totally unsuspected by the subject and any witnesses.

The operator states: "Now that you are relaxed, bring your arms together, one across the other. Fold them if you wish." Here, instead of "if you wish," the operator may specify "if you can" whenever the subject shows signs of being helpless. In that case, the operator either folds the subject's arms for him or lets them dangle loosely at his sides.

Either way, the operator continues: "Relax and rest back farther in your chair. Keep your eyes closed and look upward. Try to visualize my fingers, pressing here, against your forehead." This is a reminder of repetition of the eyelid test which served as preliminary and has been carried on at intervals, as needed. But all the while, both with the rigid arm and the hand clamp, the operator has been easing the subject farther down in his chair and tilting his head farther back, until now the subject is in a reclining position.

As the operator again presses the subject's forehead, he intones: "You will soon be deep asleep . . . . You can not open your eyes . . . . Your body is becoming powerless . . . . So powerless you can not rise . . . . You can not rise while I press your forehead . . . . You can not rise until I command you to awaken . . . . You can not rise from your chair . . . . I dare you . . . . I defy you . . . . Try!"

In this bold challenge, the operator raises his voice to a degree that may completely subdue some subjects, but is apt to antagonize others into putting all their strength into an upward struggle. If the subject gives up, fine; the operator has gained an easy victory. If not, he can still win out. As he repeats, "You can not rise . . . . I defy you . . . . Try!" he presses downward all the harder, keeping his fingers well centered against the subject's forehead and forcing his head farther back.

Since the subject's arms are folded and his legs well extended, he can not get up without first lifting his head and shoulders, which is impossible against the downward pressure of the operator's well-placed fingers. When the subject slackens his futile struggle, the operator takes advantage of it, saying, "I command you to awaken! . . . Relax! . . . You are no longer powerless . . . . Now you can arise . . . . I command it!"

With that, the operator lessens the finger pressure, even drawing his fingers completely away, while the subject comes up from his chair, usually somewhat bewildered by his brief ordeal, never suspecting the real source of the operator's repressive power. That applies most strongly when the physical, or muscular factors are taxed to the full; but it should be noted that all these tests can also be accomplished through verbal suggestions alone.

The extent to which the two factors are blended, depends upon the sincerity of the operator and the susceptibility of the subject. Some subjects accept the muscular reactions so avidly that they are practically self-hypnotized before the operator can catch up on his commands. One striking example was that of a subject who almost rolled from his chair in a hysterical effort to fight off what he thought was a hypnotic force emanating from the operator's fingertips.

Summarized, the control that the operator gains through the tests just described, or the impression that he creates—both mentally and physically—will put the subject in a perfect mood for any deeper hypnotic experiments that follow. From the operator's standpoint, these preliminaries give him an insight regarding the subject's suggestibility, which is equally helpful toward the deeper phases of hypnosis.

THE PROGRESSIVE VERBAL METHOD

We have seen how fixation can be reduced or even eliminated in favor of hypnoidal tests, which in turn are augmented by verbal suggestions to produce a true hypnotic state. That raises the question: Why not hurdle the preliminary phases and go right into verbal suggestion itself? That promptly raises another question: Can it be done?

The answer is that it can be and is being done. To be effective, however, the purely verbal method must be progressive in itself, supplanting those earlier stages with its own devices. It also depends a great deal upon a capable, persuasive operator and a highly intelligent or serious-minded subject; otherwise it may be difficult to gain undivided attention at the start.

By the same token, this method is well suited to the psychology laboratory or the medical clinic, where conditions frequently inspire confidence and cooperation. But in nearly all cases—including lectures or public demonstrations—it is apt to prove particularly effective with persons who have been hypnotized before and have shown themselves increasingly responsive to hypnotic procedures.

With such subjects, anticipation is a definite factor, which in itself supplants the usual preliminaries and enables the operator to hurdle them. Some operators may prefer to retain the fixation factor, if only briefly, and nothing may be lost thereby, even though it may not be necessary. However, both fixation and hypnoidal tests are things that the operator can introduce whenever the subject fails to respond to verbal suggestion alone.

As a typical procedure for the progressive verbal method, the operator gestures to a chair and tells the subject: "I want you to sit down. Make yourself comfortable . . . . Sit down—sit back—and relax. Sit back— lean back. Make yourself completely comfortable as you relax and lean back."

Already, the verbal suggestion has begun. Subtly, the operator has coaxed the seated subject into a reclining position which in itself is conducive to sleep. The operator follows with:

"Your mind must be comfortable, too. Dismiss all worry from your mind. Think of one thing only: Sleep . . . . You feel tired. You want to go to sleep. Your eyes are tired and you want to go to sleep . . . . Soon your eyelids will feel heavy . . . . Very heavy . . . . Your eyelids will feel very, very heavy . . . . You will want to close

81

those heavy eyelids and rest your tired eyes and go to sleep .... Just think of sleep—sleep—and close your heavy eyelids .... Sleep."

Again, the verbal suggestion is progressive, fixing the subject's mind on sleep, which is reiterated at intervals. Injected into that repeated theme is a progressive sequence wherein the subject is told that his eyes are tired, his eyelids will become heavier and heavier, and that he himself wants to go to sleep. All these points are debatable, but near enough to truth for the subject to accept them as his own ideas.

Once the subject shows signs of such acceptance, the operator should capitalize upon it; but now he guides his progressive suggestions upon the subject's own reactions, switching subtly from the future to the present tense. For example:

"You want to close your eyelids .... Close your heavy eyelids .... You are going to close your eyelids .... Close your heavy eyelids and go to sleep .... Your eyelids are closing .... Your eyelids are closed .... You are going to sleep .... Your heavy eyelids are closed .... Your head is heavy, too .... You are nodding your heavy head .... You are falling asleep .... Falling into a deep sleep .... A deep, deep sleep .... "

All this is delivered in a firm, but somewhat lulling, tone, slow enough to emphasize some words by stretching them, as "s-l-e-e-p" or "d-e-e-p s-l-e-e-p," particularly when the subject shows such symptoms. The operator's voice should be loud enough to be impressive, but not harsh or overbearing. Thus the operator can continue:

"You can hear my voice clearly .... Your eyes are

82

closed and you do not want to open them . . . . You still hear my voice, though you are falling sound asleep . . . . Sound asleep . . . . You hear my voice, but it is farther away . . . . It is becoming fainter . . . . Fainter . . . . My voice is far away, but still you hear it . . . . "

To stress this, the operator can soften his tone without lowering it, giving the illusion of distance in keeping with his words. If the subject's breathing now resembles that of sleep, the operator should time his key-words accordingly:

"Hear it while you *sleep* . . . . You hear my *voice* . . . . Nothing but my *voice* . . . . Nothing else can waken you from *sleep* . . . . Only my *voice* . . . . Can waken you from *sleep* . . . . *Sleep* . . . . "

These phrases end with the subject's outward breath, thus taking on a soothing rhythm. Repeated mention of the operator's voice establishes it in the subject's mind, eliminating any outside sounds. Most important is the operator's stressing that his voice is essential to the waking process, which thus becomes a continuation of the verbal progression, rather than a separate suggestion.

At any time the subject shows signs of awakening, or after the subject has responded to a sufficient number of tests, the operator can proceed with the awaking process, which in itself should be progressive. Having reiterated, "You will awaken only when I tell you, the operator may continue: "Soon, you will wake up feeling fine . . . . You are going to wake up when I tell you . . . . Wake up, feeling fine . . . . I am telling you now, wake up . . . . Wake up!" Then, as he notes the subject's reaction, the operator may add: "You are awake . . . .

Wide awake . . . . And feeling fine!"

Another popular way of producing the same result is to specify the moment when the subject will awaken. Here, the operator may say: "I am going to count to three. Then you will awaken . . . . Listen to my voice as I count to three . . . . One . . . . You are beginning to wake up . . . . Two . . . . You are nearly awake . . . . Three . . . . You are awake! Fully awake . . . . You are awake and feeling fine!" This has the same gradual effect found in the entire progression.

Some operators frequently extend the original hypnotic process to a point where the subject's entire body is involved, resulting in what may be termed a feeling of complete helplessness. Though slower and more prolonged, this enables the operator to work the subject into deeper stages of hypnosis, allowing more extensive tests.

Here, somewhat briefly, is such a procedure:

The operator seats the subject comfortably and tells him to relax and lean back. Adhering to that theme, the operator continues soothingly: "Just close your eyes and rest . . . . You are becoming drowsy, so relax . . . . So drowsy that your eyelids are becoming heavy . . . . So heavy that you do not want to open them . . . . Just keep those heavy eyelids closed . . . . Your head is feeling heavy, too . . . . The muscles of your face are relaxing . . . . Your mouth . . . . Your chin . . . . Your neck . . . . You can feel them tingling . . . . Restfully . . . . Comfortably . . . .

"Now your shoulders are relaxing . . . . Sinking downward . . . . Steadily . . . . Comfortably . . . . You are drowsy . . . . sleepy . . . . Your arms are relaxing now . . . . They are heavier, drawing your shoulders downward . . . . Your wrists are heavier . . . . So are your hands . . . . They are drawing your arms downward . . . . They are limp and comfortable . . . . You can feel your arms tingling . . . . Tingling comfortably . . . . From your shoulders down to your hands . . . . To your fingertips . . . . You are sleepier . . . . Sleepier . . . . "

All this while, the operator is watching the subject carefully, timing his words to the subject's reactions. At moments, he can backtrack, with comments such as: "Your eyelids are still heavy . . . . Keep them closed . . . . You want to keep them closed . . . . To rest them" —or "Relax your shoulders . . . . Let your arms draw them downward . . . . You want to rest them, so you can sleep . . . . Sleep . . . . "

Once the operator emphasizes "Sleep," he can balance it with the suggestion of "Awaken," droning, "Soon you will sleep . . . . Sleep . . . . Until you hear my voice, telling you to awaken . . . . Always, you will hear my voice, even when you sleep . . . . Only my voice can awaken you . . . . "

Thus the operator can continue with his sleep-inducing process, telling the subject, "Now your body is becoming heavy . . . . Your chest . . . . Your ribs . . . . Your hips . . . . All heavy . . . . Comfortably heavy . . . . Your back is heavy . . . . You feel a numbness moving down your spinal column . . . . Rest deep in your chair . . . . Deep in sleep . . . . Until I tell you to awaken . . . .

"Now your legs are feeling heavy . . . . Comfortably heavy . . . . Numb from your hips to your knees . . . . That heaviness is still moving downward . . . . Heavier . . . . Heavier . . . . From your knees to your ankles . . . .

Now to your feet .... So heavy, they are fixed to the floor .... Your toes are heavy .... They are tingling to their very tips .... Your whole body is asleep .... Deep in sleep .... You can not move .... You do not want to move .... Breathe easily .... Be relaxed .... Sleep .... "

The operator may stress or repeat any of these suggestions that prove necessary toward the cumulative result. Always, he is thinking ahead of the subject, so to speak; and if at any stage the subject becomes so restless or rebellious that control is threatened, a far-sighted operator will awaken the subject then and there. Thus the experiment will be scored as a success, so far as it went; and the subject will accept the fact that he was hypnotized to that same degree.

That renders the subject all the more susceptible to the verbal process, particularly if the operator stresses it during the awakening, somewhat as follows: "You are ready to awaken now .... You can move your feet and legs .... Your body is no longer numb .... You are beginning to awaken .... You hear my voice telling you to move your hands and arms .... Lift your head and awaken .... Open your eyes and wake up! .... Your eyes are open .... You are wide awake .... Eyes wide open .... Wide awake!"

The operator can backtrack to the final order as rapidly as he wants, skipping those in between. Thus, a sudden flutter of the subject's eyelids could be the operator's cue for "Wake up! Your eyes are open!" leaving the subject bewildered by the fact that his eyes are actually open and that he is wide awake. He can also speed the awakening by switching to a standard device, such as, "I am going to count to three . . . . " The whole aim is to make it convincing, so the operator can congratulate the subject on his experience and keep him looking forward to another trial.

The progressive verbal method is specially good in group hypnosis, where the operator—usually a professional hypnotist—seats as many as a dozen subjects in a row of chairs and begins to hypnotize them all at once. Since the verbal suggestions apply to all, this frequently brings very good results and helps in weeding out suitable subjects for further tests, as will be detailed later.

Similarly, when an operator finds any subject who responds easily to the verbal process, he turns it into other tests or vice versa. That is why it goes so well with other methods. The operator can "mix them or match them" as he wants, by bridging the changeovers with suitable verbal suggestions.

COUNTING METHODS

Have you ever tried to put yourself to sleep by counting up to some number—say a hundred, five hundred, a thousand, or even more? Sometimes it works, but the problem is to keep your mind from other things. That's why somebody long ago cooked up the idea of picturing a wall and counting imaginary sheep as they jump over it. Such visualization keeps the mind more strongly focussed and helps you drift into a dreamy state.

In recent years, counting as a mode of concentration has really come into its own. When you watch a spacecraft launching on the television screen, the count down of the final seconds commands increasing attention until you are oblivious to all else. At football games, spectators chant the seconds in unison with the clock: "Four—three—two—one"—to the very end of the game. Again, all eyes are riveted either on the clock or the playing field.

Such examples of auto-suggestion tie in directly with the "counting method" of hypnosis, which provides a form of "vocal fixation" in conjunction with verbal suggestion. In any of its variants this becomes a highly effective procedure, but it is usually best to experiment first with the basic method, which runs as follows:

The operator seats the subject in a chair, telling him "I want you to lean back in this chair, resting your head well back and placing your hands in front of your body. Make yourself fully comfortable, stretching your legs if you wish. Close your eyes, breathe steadily and easily; then think that you are going to sleep. Concentrate on what I tell you and it will help you to become drowsy and enjoy a quiet, restful sleep until I tell you to awaken."

This is similar to the conditioning used in the progressive verbal system, but it is more general in nature. That in itself has two advantages where certain subjects are concerned. First, it enables the operator to size up the subject and decide if he is ready to cooperate; if not, the operator can switch to a more forceful method or choose another subject. Second, so far there is no reference to counting, so when it is introduced, the subject will not recognize its importance. This helps if the subject proves impulsive and suddenly decides to resist.

The operator continues: "You will go to sleep and awaken feeling fine . . . . Just relax and feel quiet all

over . . . . Keep your eyes closed and you will get sleepy
. . . . So, so sleepy . . . . Your muscles are relaxed . . . .
You feel quiet all over . . . . Go to sleep . . . . Sleep . . . .
Sleep . . . . "

Watching the subject's eyes, the operator injects a
reminder, "Keep your eyes closed," if the subject shows
signs of opening them. Then the operator adds:

"Everything is dark to you . . . . All that you hear is
my voice . . . . You are feeling quiet from your head
down to your feet . . . . Your arms and legs are heavy
. . . . So heavy . . . . You are sleepy . . . . So sleepy . . . .
You are going to sleep . . . . By the time I count to ten,
you will be sound asleep."

Here, the operator goes into his count. It may be
steady, rhythmic, almost catching the subject off guard
and carrying him along with its suggestion. Some operators, particularly the brisk, dynamic type, prefer to use a
fast count; others, who specialize in a soothing tone,
may find a slow count more effective. In any case, the
operator's wording is essentially the same:

"One, two, three, four, five, six, seven, eight, nine,
ten . . . . You are asleep . . . . You are sound asleep . . . .
Sound asleep . . . . By the time I count five more, you
will be deeper asleep . . . . As deep asleep as you are at
dead of night . . . . As dead asleep as you are at home,
in your own bed . . . . One, two, three, four, five . . . .
You are asleep . . . . Sound asleep . . . . Dead asleep
. . . . You will stay asleep . . . . Sound asleep . . . . Until
I tell you to awaken."

The natural trend to go along with the count offsets
any reluctance that the subject may feel toward accepting the operator's orders. Once the subject is under

control, the operator clinches it with:

"You are sound asleep .... Every second your sleep is becoming deeper ....:Deeper .... Deeper .... You are having a deep, restful sleep .... Sleep quietly until I waken you .... You will not feel anything .... know anything .... hear anything, except what I tell you .... Sleep deeply until I awaken you .... Every second your sleep will become deeper .... Deeper .... Sleep until I awaken you .... "

All is now set for various tests ranging from the hypnoidal to the deep hypnotic type, as described elsewhere, dependent on the subject's responses. The best mode of awakening him is by a further count, since that idea has already been firmly planted in his subconscious. Thus the operator may tell him:

"Now, I am going to count to three .... When I count to three, you will wake up feeling fine .... Finer than you ever felt before .... Now listen to my voice .... One .... Two .... Three .... Wake up!"

When the subject's sleep is deep enough for some of the stronger tests, the operator may add before awakening him, "You will be glad you came here .... But you will not remember anything that happened." After the awakening, the operator asks the subject to recount what happened and the subject's total lack of recollection will greatly impress all the persons who witnessed the tests.

Another method is to alternate a count with verbal suggestions, combining the features of both methods in an effective way. Instead of setting a number like ten as a definite sleep target, the operator simply states, "I am going to start counting and as you listen, you will feel sleepier and sleepier, just as if you were counting yourself to sleep." Or instead, the operator can begin by asking, "Have you ever counted yourself to sleep?" and whatever the subject replies, the operator says, "I'll show you just how to do it. First, make yourself comfortable, then relax and look this way."

By "this way," the operator can mean toward his own eyes, his extended fingertips, or some object he may be holding there. He may even designate a spot on the wall or ceiling. This gives him the advantage of a slight fixation, so that he really has three forms of approach. He begins his count, injecting progressive verbal suggestions, as:

"One, two, three. You can feel yourself relaxing.... Four, five, six.... You are feeling still more comfortable. Seven, eight, nine.... You're feeling sleepy.... Sleepy.... Sleepy, more so on each number.... Ten, eleven, twelve.... Your eyelids are heavy, you want to close them.... Thirteen, fourteen, fifteen.... They are closing now.... Sixteen, seventeen, eighteen.... Closing, closing, closed.... Nineteen, your arms feel heavy.... Twenty, your legs feel heavy.... Twenty-one, your body feels heavy.... Twenty-two, heavy all over. When I reach twenty-five, you will be sound asleep.... Twenty-three, heavier. Twenty-four, heavier. Twenty-five! Sound asleep!"

Note that the operator follows the subject's inclinations just as in the progressive verbal or the direct count to ten. But by staggering the monotone of the count and the persuasion of his statements, he can prolong the process as he pleases. If the subject shows but little response as the count nears the twenties, the operator can simply announce, "When I reach the count of twenty-five, your eyelids will be closed, tightly closed"—and keep repeating that as the count continues.

At twenty-five, the operator can go into the "glued eyelid" test, telling the subject, "Your eyes are closed now, so keep them closed while you look upward . . . . Keep looking upward . . . . Now try to open your eyelids . . . . Try . . . . You can not!" He can emphasize this by pressing the subject's forehead, as in the "finger pressure" method, or by placing his thumb and fingers lightly on the subject's closed eyelids.

That enables the operator to start a new count, saying, "As I count, your eyelids will stay shut tight . . . . One, two, three . . . . Tight, tight, shut . . . . Four, five—" and so on. Then, telling the subject to relax his gaze and go to "Sleep . . . . sleep . . . . sleep . . . " the operator can lift the subject's arm and proceed with the "rigid arm test" while continuing the count. In short, any standard routine can be introduced, with repeated counts to twenty-five or any other number serving as the real persuader.

The "blink count" is another process that fits into the counting category. Actually, it is a variation of the blinking technique described under Fixation Methods. The difference is that no movement of the eyes is necessary. The subject is told to focus his attention on the operator or some object, but no fixed stare is needed. Instead, the subject is to concentrate as the operator counts, closing his eyes on "One," opening them on "Two," and so on.

Having explained that, the operator adds, "Just follow the count carefully and soon you will be falling asleep, comfortably asleep. Relax now and be ready to close your eyes: One, two, three, four, five . . . . six, seven . . . eight, nine . . . ten, eleven . . . twelve." If the subject seems to be losing count, the operator can dupe him with "Thirteen, close . . . . Fourteen, open. Fifteen, close . . . . Sixteen, open. Seventeen, close . . . . Eighteen, open. Nineteen, close . . . . Twenty, open . . . . "

Notice that either way, with or without the reminders to "close" and "open," the operator pauses longer and longer following each "odd" count; namely, while the subject's eyes are closed. This goes along with the preliminary suggestion of sleep, since the eyelids become tired by repeatedly closing and opening, so the subject naturally prefers to keep them closed. He is grateful for the pause and therefore glad when it increases, hence is apt to open them more lazily and less widely each time.

In the example just given, the operator began stretching his count early, but with some subjects a rapid count may be necessary up to twenty or beyond, before the eyelids tire. The operator watches for this and slows the beat at the proper time. He can go clear to a hundred if need be, and then begin all over, but slowly, in the same steady tone. When it reaches the point where the subject doesn't want to open his eyes at all, the operator ends the count and calmly announces: "You are falling asleep, comfortably asleep. Keep your eyes closed and relax while I count to ten. At the count of ten, you will be sound asleep. Sound asleep until I tell you to awaken."

Still watching the subject, the operator counts steadily to ten, finishing with the statement, "You are sound asleep." Usually the subject will be exactly that. When it comes to awakening the subject, the most appropriate way is to continue the counting process, with the operator announcing, "Now, I am going to count to ten again, and this time you will wake up when I reach ten." He then counts to ten and adds, "Wake up!" producing the desired result.

7

THEORY AND PRACTICE

THEORIES advanced to explain hypnotism run to two extremes: One identifies hypnosis with sleep, which would mean that practically everybody could be hypnotized; the other regards it as a form of artificial hysteria, thus limiting it to highly excitable subjects. Both of these are now obsolete, as evidenced by a modern definition of hypnotism as "an artificially induced state resembling sleep, characterized by heightened susceptibility to suggestion." This recognizes both extremes, yet allows for various in-between theories, which in turn swing from the physical to the mental.

As contrasting examples, there is the cataleptic theory, linking hypnotism with the state of immobility instinctive to many animals, which is strongly physical; and the theory of dissociation, or the separation of certain mental processes from the main stream of consciousness, sometimes resulting in a split or secondary personality. These theories, too, have not only been modified with time, but have given rise to still more complex concepts. But for practical purposes, it is interesting to note how these factors might apply to the routine of a stage hypnotist.

After calling volunteers to the stage and screening them with hypnoidal tests, the hypnotist tells a subject to stand rigidly erect, keeping his body "stiff as a plank." That done, the hypnotist continues: "Keep thinking that you are falling backward—falling backward—but I am here to catch you—" and in response to the hypnotist's magnetic passes, the subject *does* fall back and is caught as described, much to the amazement of the audience.

This is actually one of Coue's tests of auto-suggestion, in which the subject, standing as told, provides the physical factor of putting himself on so delicate a balance that the slightest sway will cause him to fall; and he adds the needed impetus mentally by letting himself go backward. No effort is needed on the hypnotist's part, but a canny operator can both speed and insure the test by placing his hands to the subject's temples and easing his body very slightly backward before going into the magnetic passes.

Making a subject stutter or stammer is another of Coue's tests, which stage hypnotists have added to their repertoire. Here, a susceptible subject is told that he can't spell or pronounce his own name, or whatever else the hypnotist orders him to say. The primary factor in this case is mental, but any slight physical impediment can be accentuated by fast talking on the hypnotist's part.

Physical and mental factors are nicely balanced in a variety of "hot and cold" tests, in which a subject recoils from the touch of the operator's forefinger, or imagines that a chair is too hot to sit in. If a susceptible subject is handed a small object and is told that it will become hotter while he holds it, he is apt to be governed by that suggestion. Here, again, it is possible to resort to trickery in the form of a brass ball, at which the subject gazes intently until it becomes so hot that he is forced to drop it.

The ball is actually made in two segments which screw together so perfectly that the join cannot be seen. It has two interior compartments, one containing water; the other, quicklime. The ball is topside up to start, but when the operator gives it to the subject, he tilts it so that the contents mingle, with the result that the metal rapidly becomes red-hot. This can prove a real convincer when an operator is confronted by a skeptical subject who refuses to let himself be hypnotized.

Conversely, a hypnotist can induce an imaginary coldness by simply touching a subject's hand or giving him some object and saying it will feel like ice. Here, a neat bit of chicanery is sometimes introduced. With a sweeping gesture, the operator points his stiffened fingers directly toward the subject's outstretched palm, commanding it to feel cold, which it instantly does. This can be repeated time and again, with any number of subjects, always with the same result, yet without actual contact.

The secret is that the sweep of the operator's hand

97

stirs up air currents that flow from his fingertips and produce the cold sensation, something that you can test on your own palm. However, one noted hypnotist used to follow this up with the near miracle of pointing his fingers toward a subject's palm at a distance of a dozen feet, yet still inducing the cold sensation. His trick was to have the subject extend his arm at a downward angle, while the operator, seated in a chair, leaned forward and pointed his fingers at about knee level. This stimulated the blood flow to the subject's hand and the resultant pulsation gave alternate sensations of cold and warmth. To augment the physical effect, the operator kept moving his fingers back and forth, timed to the pulsations, adding the mental suggestion that he was actually controlling it, thus magnifying it in the subject's mind.

Light and heavy tests are also popular. A subject is told that a chair which he has lifted will increase in weight to half a ton. Later, when he tries to pick it up, he finds he can't. This dates back to an old stage trick in which a small chest containing iron filings was placed on a pedestal which housed an electro-magnet. The subject could lift the chest easily until the juice was secretly switched on; then he became powerless.

But such devices are not needed in today's hypnotic demonstrations. By finding suitable subjects through early hypnoidal tests, they can easily be put through the paces where illusions of warmth and weight are concerned. When working with a group, there is a tendency for them to imitate one another; in short to "go along" with the act This is further encouraged by the sprinkling of stooges or trained subjects in the group;

and once the set is really rolling, the epidemic can spread through the audience.

For example, some hypnotists, after getting a whole group locked in the hand clasp test, will tell the spectators to raise their hands and clamp them; then try to get them apart. Often the majority cannot do so, until the hypnotist gives the command to relax. This, in turn further impresses the group on the platform, who by then are conditioned to go through a series of routines—individually or as a group—which constitute the main portion of the show.

A subject is given an imaginary glass and is told that it contains champagne. He goes through the motions of drinking and enjoying it. Other subjects are told that they are outdoors in a snowstorm and they proceed to button up imaginary overcoats. They are then seated in chairs and are told that they are in an automobile, which is skidding over ice and they promptly go into appropriate gyrations. They may be told that they are watching a tennis match, whereupon they begin gazing back and forth, as though they were actually there.

A subject can be told that he is out fishing and he will swing an invisible line from the end of an imaginary rod and even haul in a non-existent fish and hold it up for the audience's approval. Real objects can be used to aid and abet such tests, such as a yardstick to serve as the fishing rod; or the same yardstick may be laid on the platform and another subject told that it is a 500 pound dumb-bell which he can not possibly lift, which proves true.

A lemon can be given to a subject, who is told that it is an orange; and he will proceed to eat it without wincing. Similarly, he will eat an onion without weeping if told that it is an apple. If a cigarette is introduced as a small steel rod, a subject will be unable to bend it. Or it can be introduced simply as what it is, a cigarette, and given to a chain smoker, who is told that he will hate the taste of it. Under hypnosis, he will do just that, throwing the cigarette away after a few puffs. Here, another bit of trickery will impress a skeptical subject; if he is given a cigarette that has a horsehair inserted in it, the taste will actually be terrible.

A hypnotized subject will stroke a floor mop, believing it to be a shaggy dog; this comes under the heading of a sensory illusion. Hallucinations can also be induced; both positive and negative. In the positive type, a subject may see and pet an imaginary dog until told that it has gone away. In the negative type, he will refuse to see a real dog, if told that it is gone; and in one case, a subject actually sat down on a dog that was resting in a chair, insisting that there was nothing there.

During a hypnotic act, hypnotized subjects are told that upon awakening, they will go to sleep again when the operator commands, "Sleep!" As the show proceeds, the hypnotist suddenly shouts "Sleep!" and the subjects respond accordingly. With an orchestra present, they are told that when a certain tune is played, they will go back to sleep, which they do, when the hypnotist signals for the band to strike up.

So far, the physical and the mental have been mingled, but as a finale to the act, the hypnotist can swing to the purely physical phase by inducing what appears to be a state of complete catalepsy. He repeats the "falling test" described earlier, but commands the subject to remain rigid, which he does. The subject is then lifted by the hypnotist and an assistant, and is laid across two chair backs, his shoulders on one, the calves of his legs on the other. Two or more persons then stand upon the recumbent and subject, who bears their weight without the slightest discomfort.

All the subject has to do is arch his back and thereby support the weight. For this reason, the hypnotist uses a "horse," or a "conditioned subject" for the test, which in itself is so convincing that the audience never suspects confederacy. By gripping the back of his trousers just above the knees, the subject can apply a cantilever principle, literally turning himself into a human bridge. In cases where such a grip is not sufficient, the "horse" wears leather straps around his legs and grips those through his trousers.

In reviewing all this, it would seem that only the final cataleptic test could prove dangerous, if worked with a volunteer from the audience. But such is not the case. The real danger lurks amid those seemingly trivial tests which are so ludicrous that the audience is apt to think that the subjects are merely having fun and are not hypnotized at all. But the danger is there, due to a factor that is constantly coming more and more to the fore: Posthypnotic Suggestion.

This term does not refer to a suggestion given to a subject after he has emerged from the hypnotic state; for being no longer hypnotized, he would not be amenable to the usual type of hypnotic suggestion. By a "posthypnotic suggestion," we mean a suggestion given during the hypnotic state, which is to be fulfilled

HYPNOTISM

after the subject awakens. These posthypnotic suggestions follow two general patterns: Those which are
carry-overs from one state into the other; and those
which the subject is to follow at some specified time,
place or signal.

From the early days of hypnotism, posthypnotic
phenomena were noted, but they were identified chiefly as the second type. A subject might be told to visit
someone next week, next month, or even next year; and
when the time came, he would do so, without realizing
why. Stage hypnotists were prompt to take advantage
of this, but on a short-range basis. For instance, in the
test where a hypnotized chain-smoker would throw
away a cigarette in disgust at the operator's command,
the hypnotist would tell him that he would not smoke
again for the next twenty-four hours. Then:

Upon awakening the subject, the hypnotist would
ask him if he remembered what he had done while
hypnotized; and when the man replied, "No," the
hypnotist would offer him a cigarette and though he
accepted it eagerly, he would throw it away in disgust
the moment that he lighted it, much to his own puzzle-
ment and the amusement of the audience. For the next
day, that man would be a walking advertisement for
the hypnotist's show.

All that was harmless enough, but what many hypnotists failed to realize—and some still do!—was the
fact that during the normal course of their routine they
were implanting posthypnotic suggestions in the minds
of their subjects, unknown to themselves. For example,
the hypnotist who continually tells a hypnotized subject, "You will wake up feeling fine!" is actually using

102

a subtle form of posthypnosis. He wants the subject to "feel fine" because it will encourage other persons to let themselves be hypnotized; but actually, the awakened man may not be feeling well at all, but smiles it off because he received a command to do so.

When hypnotized subjects are told that after awakening, they will revert to the hypnotic state at the command "Sleep!" they are actually being given a posthypnotic suggestion. Some hypnotists style this "speed hypnosis" as though it were a special method of its own. Sometimes they can condition a subject to it, while he is merely in a preliminary hypnoidal state, by telling him quietly that he will go into deep sleep on command. But though seemingly harmless, this is not always so.

Take the variation where instead of commanding "Sleep!" the hypnotist has them "go under" every time they hear the orchestra play a popular tune. There is a case on record of a subject who went through that routine without realizing what had happened. Driving home after the show, he turned on the radio in his car and on came the same tune. So he went back into his trance and wrecked his car. What else could he have done?

The induced hallucinations of dogs or other animals are even more ridiculous, until they acquire the status of posthypnotic suggestions. Another well-authenticated case involved a man who was literally being hounded by a dog that no one else could even see. It finally developed that he had attended a show given by a travelling hypnotist and had volunteered as a subject. He had been put through a routine with an imag-

103

inary dog that had stayed with him from then on.

The remedy was quick, but sure. He was hypnotized by another hypnotist, who invoked the image of the phantom dog and banished it for all time. But all that could have been avoided if the original hypnotist had cleared the subject's mind at the conclusion of the session, a precaution that is regarded as a "must" by all competent hypnotists.

Any number of a variety of posthypnotic suggestions may be given by an operator to his subjects; and often these are of an immediate type, such as telling a subject to take out his wallet and keep counting his money until told to stop; or to change the positions of two empty chairs and then sit down in one of them. In private or laboratory demonstrations, subjects may be given posthypnotic suggestions pertaining to the very near future, and which can therefore be easily checked.

For example: The subject might be told to go to the post office and ask about rates on postage to Nigeria; or sent to the library to get a certain book; or to a neighbor's house to see his new dog. But should the post office be closed, or the desired book out on loan from the library, or the neighbors be away on vacation with their dog, the unfulfilled suggestion could haunt the subject like a bad dream or worse, since it is an outside association over which he has no control.

Adding the fact that a hypnotist can blank out a subject's memory of a posthypnotic suggestion, yet bring it back during another trance, it is not surprising that cases like these have raised criticism of public demonstrations of hypnotism. In some places, notably England, they have been banned, though the wisdom of such a course is debatable. Many reliable hypnotists concede that they should be licensed like practitioners in other fields; but they argue that putting an end to public exhibitions would hinder rather than help the progress of hypnotism.

It must be remembered that modern hypnotism dates from the demonstration by a professional magnetizer, Lafontaine, which roused the interest of a medical man, Braid, who conducted his own experiments from then on. In recent years, physicians and psychologists have viewed the work of professional hypnotists with similar interest, realizing that the flamboyant attitude of the stage performer, the influence of the volunteer subjects upon one another, as well as reactions of the audience, in themselves provide hypnotic conditions which are not found in a psychology laboratory, nor even in the average classroom.

Among those who made a close study of the magnetizers and drew valid conclusions from their work, was Dr. Hippolyte Bernheim, whose long years of experiment and experience involved more than 10,000 cases of hypnotic treatment; and who claimed to have successfully hypnotized 85% of his patients. The code that Dr. Bernheim established for the practice of hypnotism ran:

The following are the rules to which I believe I ought to bind myself, and to which all physicians should bind themselves before using hypnotism, in order to protect their conscience and professional honor:

First. Never hypnotize any subject without his

formal consent, or the consent of those in authority over him.

Second: Never induce sleep except in the presence of a third person in authority, who can guarantee the good faith of the hypnotizer and the subject. Thus any trouble may be avoided in the event of an accusation, or any suspicion of an attempt which is not for the relief of the subject.

Third: Never give to the hypnotized subject, without his consent, any other suggestions than those necessary for his cure. The physician has no rights but those conferred upon him by the patient. He should limit himself to the therapeutic suggestion; any other experiment is forbidden him, without the formal consent of the patient, even if it be in the interest of science. The physician should not profit by his authority over the patient in order to provoke his consent, if he thinks that the experiment which he wishes to perform may have the slightest harmful effect.

That set of rules still stands as a model and can apply to all persons who practice hypnotism in any form whatever. Even if modified for laboratory experiments or other legitimate purposes, the closer they adhere to Bernheim's standard, the better for all concerned, as our next chapter will show.

8

HYPNOTISM
AND CRIME

THE linkage of hypnotism to crime dates back to the time of Mesmer, and has not only been a controversial subject ever since, but has recently loomed to great proportions that will grow even greater. There is a twofold reason for this: Hypnotism is complex; so is modern life. Hence they find many points in common, like cogs in an intricate machine, which our minds today have truly become.

There were—and are—and probably always will be, two schools of thought pertaining to this subject:

First: Those who say that there is no danger whatever, because no person can be hypnotized against his will.

Second: Those who claim that everybody is susceptible to hypnotism in some subtle form.

To say that both are right would be as erroneous as

to say that both are wrong. The real answer lies somewhere in between and must be considered accordingly. But before delving far back into the past, or bringing things up to the present—or the future—it would be appropriate to sum up the subject from the standpoint of a real authority.

By such, we do not mean an authority on hypnotism who has given some thought to the crime angle, but an authority on criminology who has given due consideration to the hypnotic angle. The greatest by far of these was Dr. Hans Gross, justly styled "the father of criminal research," whose great work on *Criminal Investigation* sums up all possible cases in which the criminal expert has to deal with hypnotism, as follows:

It may affect the property or moral character of the person hypnotized.

Every kind of extortion may be committed with its assistance.

It may suggest crimes to be committed.

It may suggest illnesses.

The courage necessary for a crime may be suggested with its help.

Persons who have committed no crime may be unjustly accused by a person under its influence.

On the other hand, a person who has knowingly committed a crime may plead suggestion by another.

Traces of wounds and strangulations may be produced by suggestion and subsequently serve as proofs.

Abortion may be brought about by suggestion.

All kinds of illnesses—especially of the nerves, and convulsions—may be the result of illicit or awkward hypnotizing.

Involuntary suggestion may be practiced by the investigating officer himself, or other persons to be questioned.

Perhaps the earliest recorded crime case involving hypnotism was in the year 1865, when an unkempt, bearded vagrant named Thimotheus Castellan was beating his way through the French provinces posing as a magnetic healer. At one village, he exerted such strange power over a twenty-six-year-old woman named Josephine, that she went along with him in a dazed condition and acted out his commands at every place they stopped.

During those demonstrations, Josephine went from a state of complete paralysis to one of wild hysteria; and whenever people were so alarmed that they took the girl into their homes and sent Castellan on his way, she became so incoherent that they had to bring him back and let him take her with him. At last, she managed to break away on her own accord, but gave way to uncontrollable fits that brought on a fever from which she recovered under medical care.

Meanwhile, the law caught up with Castellan, and by tracing back his relations with Josephine a court adjudged him guilty of rape and sentenced him to prison, summarizing its decision with the statement: "If one puts a young girl into magnetic sleep, one can have intimate relations with her of which, when she awakens, she has no knowledge."

HYPNOTISM

Some forty years later, a much more spectacular case occurred in Germany, where a glib, personable adventurer named Czynski opened a hypnotic clinic in Dresden on the strength of a fake medical diploma. Czynski won the confidence of the wealthy Baroness von Zedlitz by hypnotizing another woman and having her diagnose the baroness's ailments while in a state of trance.

Soon, Czynski dismissed the medium and gave the baroness direct treatments on an intimate level which resulted in her seduction. Czynski squared that by subtly influencing the baroness to marry him and the ceremony was privately performed in Munich with the aid of a forged marriage license and a pretend minister. Apparently, Czynski's purpose was to retain his hold on the baroness until he could acquire the bulk of her fortune, then ditch his dupe and clear the country.

Fortunately, the Von Zedlitz family looked into the situation in time to expose the imposture. Czynski was brought to trial, but acquitted on the seduction charge, because the jury, while accepting the opinion of medical experts that hypnotism was involved, were uncertain whether the baroness had reached a state of such complete moral insensitivity that she had become a victim of "sexual bondage," as one expert termed it.

However, the jury went along with the general opinion that Czynski had used posthypnotic suggestion to promote the mock wedding, as otherwise the baroness could have recognized the fraud herself. Since that simply involved the staging of a false wedding ceremony, Czynski was found guilty only of that minor count.

Another forty years later, a still more remarkable case cropped up in Germany when a woman traveling.

on a train to Heidelberg met a man who introduced himself as "Doctor Bergen" and remarked that she looked ill, which she was. He offered to give her treatments in Heidelberg, so she visited him at intervals and soon came under his spell. When the self-styled "Dr. Bergen" began extorting money from the woman, her husband complained to the police, who were unable to locate Bergen. However, since his treatments had obviously involved hypnosis, they called in a physician, Dr. Ludwig Mayer, who specialized in hypnotism, and he began to unravel a very strange case.

Since the woman could not recall exactly where she had gone for the "treatments," nor locate other places where she had accompanied Bergen during their somewhat clandestine relationship, Dr. Mayer surmised that the impostor had used posthypnotic suggestion to create mental blocks in her mind, thus effectively covering up his trail, should she be questioned. So he put the woman into repeated trances, during which he suggested "flashbacks" to the Bergen episodes, only to run into the very obstacles that he anticipated.

Painstakingly, Dr. Mayer continued his hypnotic treatment over many months; and whenever he ran into an odd expression like "Leichtbion" or "Comarus" or "Exiton," he kept questioning the woman regarding it. Finally, like a cryptanalyst breaking a complex international code, Dr. Mayer discovered that those were the "key-words" by which Bergen had made the woman forget what he had told her, insofar as any other trance state might be involved.

So Dr. Mayer began seeking lesser associations for those words, such as where or when Bergen had spoken them; what he looked like when he uttered them, and so on. Gradually, he pieced together enough data for the police to pick a suspect answering that description, who had on occasion falsely posed as a doctor, only to have him deny emphatically that he was Dr. Bergen, or had ever heard the name.

But the capable Dr. Mayer had scored too many hits for the pretended Dr. Bergen to dodge them. In one trance, the woman had described a swimming pool where she had been with Bergen; and although the police had been unable to follow up that lead, she had also given a detailed description of a fancily embroidered towel that Bergen had brought with him to the pool. Once the police had their suspect in custody, they searched his apartment and found the very towel that his dupe had remembered.

While piecing together the woman's past during her retroactive trance states, Dr. Mayer had gathered that Bergen had sometimes written her notes with orders to destroy them; and later, by use of his key-words, had caused her to forget their contents. But Dr. Mayer had countered that by hypnotizing his patient, handing her a blank sheet of paper and telling her that it was a Bergen message that she had forgotten to destroy. To prove it, Dr. Mayer had told her to read it aloud and she had, thus providing a clue to a time when she had met Bergen, as well as naming the place.

The ultimate reason for all this, according to data finally gathered by the police, was to get rid of the woman's husband. On six different occasions, as revealed through Dr. Mayer's transcripts, she had made abortive attempts to kill him at Bergen's order. The woman's husband was able to furnish corroborative evidence on that score, particularly in regard to two poison attempts which had made him sick; and a time when his motorcycle brakes had failed, nearly resulting in a fatal crash. But in no case had he suspected anything at the time.

At one point, the pretended Dr. Bergen, to make sure his posthypnotic suggestions were working out, had introduced the duped woman to a man posing as a detective, who had questioned her regarding her recent actions. Dr. Mayer uncovered that fact, too, so when the accomplice was identified and taken into custody along with Bergen, their game was really through. Found guilty on various charges, the man known as Bergen was sentenced to ten years in prison; and his accomplice was sent up for four years.

Such criminal potentials were foreseen and tested in the early days of hypnotism. Bernheim tells how Professor Liegeois, who taught law in Nancy, fired a revolver and hit a target; then loaded it again and handed it to a young woman who had frequently been hypnotized by Dr. Liebault, without telling her that the charge was actually blank. He suggested that she shoot and kill a local magistrate whom she did not like.

Not only did she obey the command, she did so in the presence of the local police commissioner, who happened to be present; and when the magistrate rolled over and played dead as part of the act, the woman calmly confessed the crime and expressed no regrets. When asked directly by Professor Liegeois whether he had suggested the "murder," she replied emphatically that he had not; and insisted that it had been her own idea throughout.

Bramwell describes a case where he hypnotized a highly religious and respectable shopkeeper before a medical society in York, England, and suggested that he act the part of a dissenting minister preaching a sermon, which he refused to do. He was then told to play the part of a fish peddler, which he also refused, as one role to him was disrespectful, the other beneath his dignity. When told to play the part of a circus ring-master, he did so, willingly, introducing the doctors as animals in a zoo, and having real fun doing it.

Recognizing the man's strict compunctions, Bramwell on another occasion showed him a lump of sugar telling him that it was loaded with enough arsenic to kill a dozen people. Bramwell then dropped the sugar in a cup of tea and told the man to give it to a friend of his who had entered the room. Instead of showing the outraged repugnance that Bramwell expected, the man did exactly as ordered. When Bramwell exclaimed, "Do you realize that you have poisoned your friend?" the man shrugged and laughed: "Why not? He has lived long enough."

Despite such demonstrations, there arose a wide-spread opinion that no hypnotized person could be induced to commit a criminal act; that something in the inner mind would rebel before the crucial moment. Tests like those described by Bernheim and Bramwell were discounted on the ground that the subjects knew that they were hypnotized and therefore only play-acting. The fact that the same subjects were hypnotized over and over, thereby becoming conditioned to the fact, was also cited as evidence that they knew what it was all about.

In fact, one stock hypnotic stunt was to hand a subject a paper dagger and tell him to stab someone with it at a specified time. Acting in accordance with the post-hypnotic suggestion, the subject would usually do so. But it was generally conceded that if, when the time came, he should be given a genuine dagger instead of the fake one, he would recoil from the deed.

That argument, however, defeated itself to a marked degree. Assuming that, as claimed, the hypnotized subject still was sufficiently aware of his actions to control them inwardly, he could originally have recognized the paper dagger for what it really was, thereby subconsciously accepting the whole suggestion as a harmless pretence. Given a real dagger later, he could, by the same token, note the difference and naturally realize that something was wrong and should be corrected.

Over the course of years, many authorities have come to a middle course in relation to crime and hypnotism. Granting that a subject has an inner sense that enables him to rebel instinctively if asked to commit an illegal or immoral act while hypnotized, there is still the question: Just what does that particular subject regard as illegal or immoral?

In today's complex world, that question looms large enough to put a whole new perspective on hypnotism, as with many other matters. Where one person today may regard law and order as the twin pillars of legality and morality, another may measure them in terms of civil disobedience. With such extremes in accepted standards, almost anybody may do almost anything,

HYPNOTISM

That was foreseen, back around 1895, by George Du Maurier, whose novel, *Trilby*, involved the misadventures of a heroine of that same name, who came under the hypnotic spell of a bearded musician named Svengali, who aspired to be a great singer, but whose voice was nothing more than a harsh croak. Finding that Trilby had a fine voice, but that she was tone deaf, Svengali, through his mesmeric power, turned her into a human puppet who sang the magnificent tunes that were roving through his talented but demented brain.

It was the Castellan story all over, but on a grander and more lavish scale, reaching its climax when Svengali, whose influence was more baneful than beneficial, died from a heart attack, ending Trilby's career as a proxy nightingale, with her own death following soon after. Superficially, Trilby's plight resembled that of the Baroness Von Zedwitz, whose case was at that time attracting public notice, with even the name Czynski approximating that of Svengali, the bearded hypnotist of fiction.

Back in the year when Castellan went rampant, a novel appeared with the title *From the Earth to the Moon*, by a French author named Jules Verne, who today is regarded as the father of science-fiction. But Verne's incredible notion of projecting a spacecraft to the moon and back was outmatched by Du Maurier's concept of a bearded mystic who could exercise hypnotic power to the point of life and death, not only when his entranced subject was close at hand, but by remote control. Confirmed skeptics whimsically agreed that when men did finally reach the moon, a real life Svengali would probably crop up from somewhere; but that was just another way of

116

saying that neither of those things could ever happen.

Then, along in the summer of 1969, the incredible happened when three American astronauts landed on the moon and later returned safely to earth. But almost on the eve of the ticker tape parade that welcomed the astronauts to New York, the nation was shocked by one of the most hideous and senseless mass murders ever recorded. In Hollywood, a rising young actress, Sharon Tate, and four guests in her posh $200,000 mansion were found slain in what appeared to be a ritualistic murder, in which the bodies were roped with nylon cords and hacked beyond recognition.

At first, the trend was to blame the participants, saying that only freaks and weirdos would have attended such a bash. All the idiosyncracies of the murder victims were magnified to the point where all sorts of bizarre theories were proposed. A true crime writer came up with the opinion that a frustrated member of the party had left early, then returned later with a gun, and in a dope-crazed mood had rubbed out the merry-makers one by one. A so-called psychic detective went over the scene and presumably through extrasensory perception gained the impression that some mock ceremony had backfired and that members of the group had turned it into the real thing and then fled.

Police, meanwhile, were trying to link the Tate massacre to a double-knife murder of a chain store magnate and his wife, which occurred the next night and had points in common with the earlier crime, including one pointed clue, the word "Pigs" scrawled in blood at each murder scene. It was possible that one crime was simply a copy of the other, done by someone who had read about the earlier case; but investigators gained a break from the still earlier murder of a young musician. A girl being held for complicity in that crime began talking to a cellmate, telling her details of the Tate massacre as well. The cellmate informed the police and the whole sordid story began to unfold.

All those murders—and more—were done at the express order of a bearded leader of a hippie group or "family" that roved from one rendezvous to another, their principal headquarters being an old and much neglected ranch, which had once been used as a movie set for Western pictures. There, they brought stolen cars, selling some and converting others into dune buggies, meanwhile engaging in wild, drug-inspired rituals and long-range sexual orgies. When they ran out of cash, they salvaged food from trash and garbage cans, a job usually allotted to a few of the two dozen girls who cohabited promiscuously with the bearded master and his half-dozen male associates.

Known affectionately as "Satan" to his hippie cult, this self-appointed Devil of the Dunes transported his slaphappy harem from one outpost to another in a beaten-down bus; but between times, he shaved his beard and made forays into the outside world, where he tried to sell his musical talents, which had considerable merit, but apparently lacked commercial possibilities. This, according to the self-styled Satan's subordinates —however true or false their testimony might be—embittered him against the Establishment, otherwise known as the existing power structure.

Back in his desert retreat, the master of the devil cult soon reverted to his Satanic self, beard and all. There, he preached a garbled gospel of hate toward all "pigs," meaning affluent people who thrived under the Establishment; and particularly those who refused to further his musical ambitions. At the ranch, he played the Svengali role in real life, far beyond the fictional concept, for he operated on a wholesale basis, with dozens of puppets ready to do his bidding. True, he had the advantage of LSD and marijuana, which he doled out to his "Family" as required; but the old hypnotic spell was still his chief forte.

According to one report, the Tate massacre was purely coincidental, as the Svengali of the Sands actually held a grudge against the head of a recording company who had rented the lavish mansion earlier. After the case was broken, the attorney for one of the girls who had participated in the raid, stated that she and all the rest had been under the modern Svengali's hypnotic control and that they had followed his overpowering suggestions by going to the estate clad entirely in black, entering exactly as he had ordered, and turning the place into a shambles.

The fact that their Satanic master did not accompany them was strong proof of his posthypnotic power; and this was confirmed later when the girl was quoted as saying that she and the rest of The Family belonged entirely to him and not to themselves, so when he ordered them to kill everyone in the mansion as a symbol of protest against "piggies," they had gone through with it automatically. She admitted that they were all on "acid"—a term for LSD—but that the more they stabbed, the more they liked it, much like making love; and that they continued the stabbing to gruesome lengths in order to release the souls of the victims.

All that smacked of the warped religious hodge-podge dished out by the Supersvengali, though how well the testimony of an admittedly hopped-up witness would stand up in court was something that remained to be seen. Later investigation indicated that the follow-up murder of the chain store owner and his wife was practically a random choice in an exclusive neighborhood where any and all were "pigs," so it really didn't matter. On that occasion, the master mind allegedly led the raid himself, but with his followers already hypnotically conditioned for the subordinate parts they were to play.

As evidence piled up against The Family, linking the group to earlier murders, the bearded leader and his remaining followers were rounded up at their isolated hideout above Death Valley, some two dozen being booked on charges of car thefts. Their statements were pieced with those of ex-members of The Family, thus forming a more detailed picture of the whole bizarre business, and the hypnotic factor in particular.

One youth, who allegedly led the raid at the Tate mansion, was quoted as saying that their bearded leader was an insane genius, yet capable of real miracles; and that his followers, who regarded themselves as Satan's Slaves, were truly under a hypnotic spell. He believed he was a superman; and so did his followers. When he fed them more suggestions, they followed him.

According to this account, the self-styled Satan would say, "I need a car," and someone would go out and steal one. If he said to a follower, "I need money," that member of the group would go and get it; no matter how. He was described as literally putting on a hypnotic act, but far more effective than any that were seen at night clubs, for this modern Svengali seemingly could project commands mentally or read the minds of his subjects. That was confirmed by a feminine member of The Family, who insisted that she could feel the influence of her Satanic master, even though he was in a jail cell 200 miles away.

All this was a flashback to the days of Mesmer, when the fixed gaze was used to induce hypnosis. The subject stared at a bright object, namely, the operator's eyes, and thus was hypnotized. But the operator, in his turn, was staring at the subject's eyes and thus became mildly hypnotized, establishing a *rapport* between their minds, according to some authorities. But the mesmeric theory has been pretty well discarded in favor of posthypnosis, which could definitely apply in the present case. Both the automatic commission of a crime and the feeling of being controlled by someone far away, have the earmarks of a previously implanted impression.

One girl who had belonged to the desert Family, but had luckily shaken off its shackles, was quoted as saying that its hard core consisted of an "in group" that none of the ordinary members could join until they had gone on a murder raid. She claimed that the bearded leader used murder simply to keep his fanatical followers in line, since anyone who left would either be killed by members of the cult or turned over to the police. When ordered to go on a murder raid, this informant had managed to duck out soon enough and get far enough away to escape both hazards.

Talk of an "in group" with murder as its aim is a matter of history repeating itself on an even more fantastic scale, dating back nearly a thousand years to the notori-

121

ous Hassan Sabbah, who established himself in a mountain stronghold in Persia, where he became known as the "Old Man of the Mountain" and—with his successors— held a fantastic control over a group of fanatically dedicated followers. Two words were coined from the name Hassan, one being "hashish," a drug derived from the hemp plant, like marijuana; and "assassin," denoting a ruthless murderer, who originally was stirred to action through the use of such a drug.

Legend has it that Hassan turned their pipe dreams into seeming reality by establishing a fake paradise within his mountain fortress, where his chosen followers— representing the "in group" of their day—could indulge in all forms of sensual pleasures, providing only that they would kill at the grand master's order. That they did, assassinating the heads of many governments, with total disregard for their own safety, firm in the belief that if they were executed for their crimes, they would find a permanent paradise as exquisite as the one that they had tasted.

After a few centuries, this widespread organization, whose real purpose was known only to the chosen few, was stamped out, but its scattered members went underground and persisted as smaller groups up until modern times, and small remnants of the assassin cult are said to exist in the mountains of Syria, even today.

But assassination, itself, has continued steadily through changing times and in many climes. Usually, political assassinations are so widely spaced that the furore of one has died before another occurs, so that each seems like an isolated or even a unique event. But a study of the subject shows the opposite to be true. Over a prolonged period prior to World War I., major political assassinations in Europe struck an average of one a year, culminating in the slaying of an Austrian archduke that triggered the war itself.

If we include all the minor cases before and since that time; then add on the many attempted assassinations that were foiled, the number becomes legion, and it becomes apparent that assassins are as active as ever; perhaps more than ever. Further survey shows that many of these political slayings follow a set pattern, just as they did in yore. Usually, they involve stolid slayers, determined in their task, ready to take the consequences and convinced that they, not their victims, are the real martyrs.

This is particularly true in the sequence of assassinations involving American presidents, to the point where the hypnotic factor may be strongly involved. John Wilkes Booth, who assassinated Abraham Lincoln, was a vainglorious actor whose dramatic poses could well have been a form of self-hypnosis. In addition, he unquestionably exerted a persuasive hypnotic power over the unfortunate dupes whom he enlisted as his fellow-conspirators, and who paid the death penalty as a result. One in particular, Atzerodt, went to the gallows as if still in a trance.

Charles Guiteau, who assassinated James Garfield, was a man in an almost perpetual hypnoidal or hypnotic state, who kept hearing spirit voices telling him to commit the crime. Leon Czolgosz, slayer of William McKinley, affords another case with probable hypnotic overtones. In recent years, it has been suggested that Lee Harvey Oswald was under some strange control when he assassinated John Kennedy; while Jack Ruby, who shot down Oswald in retaliation, must have been in something of a hypnotic mood to commit the deed not only in public but before TV cameras on a national hook-up.

It is a known fact that Sirhan Sirhan, who assassinated Senator Robert Kennedy, often put himself into hypnotic trances by staring at his own eyes in a mirror set between two lighted candles. His notebook showed orders that he had apparently written automatically, another indication of a hypnotic state. At the time of the assassination, Sirhan entered an alcove that had mirrors reflecting dazzling lights, which according to one authority, could have produced a flashback to his tests in self-hypnosis, inducing the dissociated state responsible for the crime.

Most singular, however, is the fact that Sirhan himself came from the general region of Asia Minor where the last stray members of the thousand-year old assassin cult still has its secret adherents. Whether or not the baleful influence of the Old Man of the Mountain still shapes the minds and purposes of people inhabiting that region is a question in itself. Plausibly, something in Sirhan's youth could have caused his later motivation; yet it may merely have been coincidence that he should have come from there. Still, strange things can always happen when hypnotism is involved.